Decades of American History

AMERICA IN THE 1970s

BREE BURNS

☑® **30519007449088**
Facts On File, Inc.

A Stonesong Press Book
Decades of American History: *America in the 1970s*

Facts On File, Inc.
132 West 31st Street
New York NY 10001

Library of Congress Cataloging-in-Publication Data

Burns, Bree
 America in the 1970s / Burns, Bree.
   p. cm.—(Decades of American history)
 "A Stonesong Press book."
 Includes bibliographical references and index.
 ISBN 0-8160-5643-9
 1. United States—History—1969—Juvenile literature.
2. Nineteen seventies—Juvenile literature. I. Title. II. Series.
 E855.B87 2005
 973.924—dc22

                                        2005013667

Facts On File books are available at special discounts when purchased in bulk quantities
for businesses, associations, institutions, or sales promotions. Please call our Special Sales
Department in New York at (212) 967-8800 or (800) 322-8755.

You can find Facts On File on the World Wide Web at http://www.factsonfile.com

Text design by Laura Smyth, Smythetype
Photo research by Sarah Parvis
Cover design by Pehrsson Design

Printed in the United States of America

VB PKG 10 9 8 7 6 5 4 3 2 1

This book is printed on acid-free paper.

CONTENTS

Chapter 1
THE 1970s BEGIN, 1970–1971 • 5

Chapter 2
DARKNESS DESCENDS ON THE WHITE HOUSE, 1972–1974 • 21

Chapter 3
THE 1970s BEGIN AGAIN, 1974–1975 • 43

Chapter 4
CARTER COMES TO WASHINGTON, 1976–1977 • 57

Chapter 5
ADDRESSING HUMAN RIGHTS, 1977–1978 • 73

Chapter 6
OPTIMISM, ESCAPISM, AND DISILLUSIONMENT, 1978–1979 • 87

Chapter 7
THE 1970s WIND DOWN, 1979 • 99

GLOSSARY • 120

FURTHER READING • 122

INDEX • 124

CHAPTER 1

THE 1970s BEGIN, 1970–1971

AS THE DECADE OF THE 1970S BEGAN, a postage stamp cost 6¢. A loaf of bread was 24¢; a quart of milk was $1.32. The average income for an individual was $3,900; for an entire household, $8,933. There were 203 million people living in the United States, and the country was emerging from one of the most turbulent decades in its history. At times, it seemed like a quiet decade compared to the 1960s. However, it was actually a time of violence and political unrest. It was also a decade of positive changes and many firsts. For example, the decade marked the first time both an African-American woman and a Jewish woman were elected to Congress.

Protests against the Vietnam War continued into the 1970s. *(Lyndon Baines Johnson Library and Museum)*

Richard Milhous Nixon remains one of the most controversial political figures in 20th-century American history. *(Library of Congress)*

"Television brought the brutality of war into the comfort of the living room. Vietnam was lost in the living rooms of America—not on the battlefields of Vietnam."

—Marshall McLuhan, sociologist

An African-American woman ran for president for the first time. Three major cities elected their first African-American mayors. It was the first time human beings saw what the surface of Mars looked like, when a Viking mission to Mars sent back digital pictures. It was also the first time a U.S. president resigned from office.

In 1969, Richard Milhous Nixon had been sworn in as 37th president of the United States. During Nixon's presidency, the White House and the presidency itself would come under attack in a way they never had before. Nixon remains one of the most controversial individuals of the 20th century.

When Nixon took office, the United States was painfully divided about its involvement in the Vietnam War, in which U.S. forces supported one side of a civil war in a small Southeast Asian nation on the other side of the world. The United States supported the non-Communist forces based in South Vietnam; the North Vietnamese sought to unite all the Vietnamese under Communist rule. After being elected, Nixon deepened U.S. involvement in Vietnam. There were other aspects of his foreign policy though that helped create his enduring legacy. Nixon re-established friendly relations with the Communist governments of the Soviet Union (détente) and so-called Red China, two major world powers that had long been considered enemies of the United States during the cold war.

Nixon's personal style remains a point of contention: Nixon was either a determined political genius or a sneak and a criminal, depending on point of view. Decades after he resigned the presidency, Richard Nixon's life and career are still under examination.

PEACE WITH HONOR

The war in Vietnam was at the center of U.S. politics as the 1970s began. During his campaign for president, Nixon declared that he would end the war, though he insisted that peace must be achieved with honor. Those against the war believed that U.S. troops should be brought home immediately. They saw Nixon's peace with honor position as introducing unnecessary delay. At Nixon's inauguration, antiwar protestors threw eggs and displayed the flag of the Communist Soviet Union. This was extremely offensive to Nixon, who was a life-long anticommunist.

Eighty-one antiwar protestors were arrested at the inauguration, which has been described as a terrible low point in U.S. history. Prior to 1969, presidential in-augurations were dignified scenes; Americans would never have thought such disorder at an inauguration possible.

Nixon identified himself with hardworking, middle-class Americans. He firmly believed that most Americans, a group he referred to as the Silent Majority, supported his policies. In contrast, Nixon referred to students protesting the Vietnam War as "bums." His contempt for his opponents earned him many enemies.

A U.S. Army helicopter hovers above Vietnamese air force troops. Although the U.S. forces were far better supplied and equipped than their opponents, helicopters did not help in guerrilla fighting in the jungle, at which the Viet Cong excelled. *(U.S. Department of Defense)*

"It seems like a nightmare but this is real. I've really been shot!"

—Alan Canfora, one of the students wounded at Kent State

KENT STATE PROTEST

On April 30, 1970, just as the new decade began, President Richard Nixon announced to a national television audience that U.S. troops were invading Cambodia, the country west of Vietnam through which the North Vietnamese military was supplying their troops in the South. In reality, the U.S. had been conducting bombing raids in Cambodia for more than a year, but it had been kept secret from the public. This was in direct contradiction to what Nixon had been promising for the entire year: to replace U.S. troops with newly trained South Vietnamese soldiers and bring the troops home.

A few days after Nixon's speech, more than 350 college campuses exploded in protest over Nixon's speech and the U.S. invasion of Cambodia. On the campus of Kent State University, in Ohio, student protestors set fire to the Reserve Officers Training Corp (ROTC) building. The governor called in the National Guard, who opened fire on the students. The shooting lasted 25 seconds. When it was over, 4 protestors were dead and 9 others were wounded. Many of the victims were bystanders.

Students had been protesting the war on college campuses since the 1960s, but nothing like this had happened before. "It was representative of a country gone mad," wrote historian Stephen Ambrose. "American troops shot down American students who were changing classes."

General William C. Westmoreland, the top commander of troops in Vietnam, led an army of young men who had predominantly been drafted into the service; there were few volunteers. *(Lyndon Baines Johnson Presidential Library and Museum)*

INHERITING VIETNAM

Little that occurred during the late 20th century caused as much emotion as the war in Vietnam. Almost as soon as President Lyndon Johnson sent in combat troops during the 1960s, citizens were condemning the action as unjust and calling for the immediate withdrawal of troops. Others believed that it was a citizen's duty to support the actions of their government and

Americans associated with the antiwar movement were also linked with the counterculture that had begun in the 1960s.
(Lyndon Baines Johnson Presidential Library and Museum)

that it was akin to treason to question the justness or unjustness of the government's actions. The United States was divided between the Hawks, or those who supported the war, versus the Doves, who opposed it. Supporters of the war suggested that if South Vietnam fell to the Communists, neighboring countries in Asia, and later elsewhere, would also become Communist and fall under the political sphere of the Soviet Union. This was known as the *Domino Theory.* The Doves criticized the war as lacking clear military objectives, exacting a huge cost monetarily, and costing thousands of young Americans their lives—all to support the government of a small country on the other side of the world.

The top U.S. commander in Vietnam was General William Westmoreland. His forces were composed of young men who had been drafted into the army. They had not chosen to enroll but instead had been chosen by lottery. Westmoreland led this army full of young

18-YEAR OLDS GIVEN THE RIGHT TO VOTE

The Twenty-sixth Amendment to the U.S. Constitution was ratified on July 1, 1971, extending voting rights vote to 18-year-olds. In the year immediately prior, many in the United States had complained that 18-year-olds could be drafted into the military and sent off to die for their country, yet they were not allowed to vote for the politicians who might send them there, as the voting age was 21. President Nixon certified the amendment in a signing ceremony at the White House.

Though he was a staunch anticommunist, President Nixon re-established friendly relations with both Communist China and the former Soviet Union. His visit to the Great Wall of China was the first by a U.S. president. *(Nixon Presidential Materials)*

"Vietnam was the first war ever fought without any censorship. Without censorship, things can get terribly confused in the public mind."

—General William C. Westmoreland, top commander of U.S. troops in Vietnam

men to battle in an environment that was totally alien to them. There was no clear front to the conflict; the enemy could be hiding anywhere in the jungle. Life was an ordeal. Drugs and other stimulants filtered their way into the routine of many servicemen, and morale was very low.

In many ways, Americans were divided about the war along class lines. To some it appeared that working class youth—the children of the Silent Majority— were the ones fighting in Vietnam, while college students were exempt from the draft and had the luxury to protest. Many of the young men who fought in Vietnam were from poor families who lacked connections that could get them exempted from the draft.

Images of the war in Vietnam were broadcast every day into the nation's homes on television, which had not been readily available during earlier military conflicts. This helped to galvanize a growing antiwar movement. Opponents of the war often rejected the "Establishment," or prevailing cultural norms, in politics, attire, and appearance. Youth culture and political protest seemed to have become intertwined, with many young protestors growing their hair long, and adapting an alternative lifestyle that embraced drugs, free love, and rock music, in addition to protest, as part of a "counter-culture" that had begun in the 1960s. Of course, this was a stereotype, as people from all segments of U.S. society were among those opposing the war.

The Nixon administration did not have a favorable opinion of the youth culture. Nixon's vice president, Spiro T. Agnew, verbally attacked not only students but also professors, news reporters, and the movies and music of the day that questioned the legitimacy of U.S. involvement in Vietnam.

Even Americans who opposed the war for pragmatic reasons, such as economic costs, were often uncomfortable with the antiwar movement of the period. The young antiwar leaders of the early 1970s became increasingly aggressive, sometimes greeting returning soldiers with jeers and taunts and spitting on troops in airports and on public streets. A unique situation arose in which many Americans supported the antiwar cause but opposed the style of antiwar leaders, their methods, and their manner of protest.

> *"If the Mets can win the World Series, the United States can get out of Vietnam."*
>
> —Tom Seaver, 1969 World Series winning pitcher, New York Mets

Disney World opened in Orlando, Florida, in 1971.

ALL IN THE FAMILY

The immensely popular situation comedy *All in the Family* changed the course of television comedy, which had always shown fairly idealized family situations up to that point. *All in the Family* depicted a contemporary household at odds—much like the country itself. The storylines followed Archie Bunker, a conservative dock foreman, who lived in Queens, New York, with his wife Edith, his daughter Gloria, and her liberal husband, Mike Stivic, a sociology graduate student.

Archie called Mike "meathead" at every opportunity. He and Mike were on opposite sides of the fence on every social and political topic. They argued about everything from Vietnam to food. Edith and Gloria were often in opposition to their husbands, and even each other, when it came to their roles as women—both in their home and in society. The Bunkers and Stivics conflicted with each other on the hot topics of the time—war, race relations, abortion, and more. However, the show never forgot to remind the audience of the deep feelings the characters had for each other. No matter which character viewers might identify with more, every character was presented with affection.

All in the Family changed the nature of situation comedies, opening them to realistic characters, mature themes, and adult dialogue. It showed how narrow-minded both conservatives and liberals could be and let could find humor amid the turmoil. The show ran from 1971 to 1983.

The environmental movement gained popularity in the early 1970s as Earth Week was celebrated in 1970, and Earth Day was recognized by the United Nations in 1971 to remind people of the shared responsibility to protect Earth's natural resources.

THE ENVIRONMENTAL MOVEMENT

In the early 1970s, public concern about pollution, waste reduction, and the extinction of endangered species grew. The energy crisis forced prices for gas and oil sky high, spurring the investigation of alternative sources of energy. The environmental movement was a response to these issues.

The idea of ecological awareness, an awareness of relations between living things and their environment, took hold during the early 1970s. The concept of getting back to nature flourished. Organic food, grown without human-developed pesticides and fertilizers and prepared without preservatives or synthetic flavoring or coloring, became popular. An organic lifestyle became a popular choice for many during the decade. Vegetarian diets, growing one's own food, wearing clothing from all-natural fibers, and using all-natural products found favor with a large number of people.

Books about ecology, conservation, and living a natural lifestyle, such as *The Whole Earth Catalog,* were important in spreading these ideas. The first Earth Day, promoting environmental awareness, took place on April 22, 1970. The United Nations recognized an International Earth Day in 1971, on the first day of spring.

The ecology flag was a symbol of the environmental movement in the 1970s. Although the flag itself was not widely popular, the movement continued and grew stronger and larger throughout the rest of the decade. *(Sarah Parvis)*

MUSIC AND THE YOUTH MOVEMENT

The term *generation gap* referred to the concept that there were many differences between the attitudes of young people and those of their parents' age and older. These differences seemed to encompass just about anything. The young and old clashed on politics, ideologies, appearance, employment, drugs, sex, and even who their favorite entertainers were. Protest music also contributed to the gulf between young and old. Edwin Starr's song "War" was number 10 on the Top 40 chart for 1970; John Lennon released the song "Give Peace a Chance," while Marvin Gaye sang in "What's Going On," "there are too many of you dying."

As the 1960s faded into the 1970s, there was a changing of the guard in contemporary popular music. Within a year of each other, three icons of the youth movement died from what were considered drug-related causes. On September 18, 1970, pioneering rock guitarist Jimi Hendrix died in London at age 27. Twenty-seven-year-old rock singer Janis Joplin died on October 4, 1970, of complications from a drug overdose, and Jim Morrison, lead singer of The Doors, was 27 when he died in Paris, France, on July 3, 1971.

All three of these musicians embodied a provocative, rebellious image in their personas, and all three were regarded as outspoken innovators in their field. Their deaths at a young age were among the first to occur among the generation of 1960s rock stars. Subsequently, many successful artists in the world of popular music tended to be of a blander and less revolutionary nature. This was a trend that would continue throughout the decade with so-called easy-listening artists topping the pop music charts and the rise of disco.

THE RISE OF IDENTITY POLITICS

Building on the progress of the civil rights movement of previous decades, many groups outside the mainstream

Michael Jackson, age 13, scored his first solo hit with 1971's "Got To Be There."

Jimi Hendrix's unorthodox guitar style influenced musicians throughout the 1970s and into the 21st century. (*Photofest*)

Popular music in the 1970s was driven by sales of vinyl records and eight-track or cassette tapes. Singles were on turntables at 45 rpm. Albums, or LPs, played at 33$\frac{1}{3}$.

In 1970, the National Football League and American Football League merged into one league.

Thurgood Marshall was the first African American appointed to the U.S. Supreme Court. *(Lyndon Baines Johnson Presidential Library and Museum)*

began to examine their place in American culture. As individuals with common ethnic backgrounds or social identity banded together in identifiable groups, a movement of identity politics was born. For example, African Americans, Americans Indians, gays, women, and others focused on how their particular groups were represented in media and affected by politics.

AFRICAN AMERICANS IN THE MAINSTREAM

The 1970s saw a decline in the prominence of African-American radical groups and provided an opportunity for more moderate African-American leaders. Thurgood Marshall, the first African American appointed to the U.S. Supreme Court, demonstrated the possibilities for working within the political system. The formation of the Congressional Black Caucus provided African-American U.S. representatives with the means to determine priorities of racial reform. The National Black Political Convention, held in 1972 in Gary, Indiana, was attended by 8,000 delegates and marked an effort to broaden African-American participation in discussions of political alternatives. In that year Representative Shirley Chisholm, a Democrat from New York, became the first African-American woman to run for the presidential nomination of a major political party.

While African-American leaders focused on gaining equal education and economic opportunities for their constituents, there was a growing cultural awareness of African heritage among many African Americans. African-American pride influenced members of other ethnic groups as well. People joined ethnic political organizations, participated in ethnic neighborhood celebrations, and learned the traditions of their ancestors. Colleges broadened their course offerings, granting degrees in fields including women's studies, Jewish studies,

BLAXPLOITATION

The term *blaxploitation* was first used by *New York* magazine in 1972 to describe the film *Superfly*. The word describes a short-lived film genre targeted at African Americans. In the 20th century, film roles for African Americans had been limited, often fulfilling racial stereotypes. The civil rights movement helped to overthrow some of those stereotypes, and Sidney Poitier became the first African American to win a major Academy Award for his performance in *Lilies of the Field* in 1963.

Blaxpoitation films were often over the top affairs with lots of action and soundtracks featuring popular musical genres such as soul, rhythm and blues, and funk. Some critics say that blaxploitation films glorified urban drug culture and violence, but to moviegoers the actors became new icons. Many were made by white directors, but black directors such as Melvin Van Peebles also worked in the genre. Some of the most memorable blaxploitation films include: *Cotton Comes to Harlem* (1970), *Shaft* (1972), *Superfly* (1972), *Blacula* (1972), *Cleopatra Jones* (1973) and *Black Caesar* (1973). Eventually, approximately 150 films were produced in this genre.

---

and black studies. Ethnic awareness and pride turned out to be a real force for change during the 1970s.

THE WOMEN'S MOVEMENT

Women were a major force for social and political change in America during the 1970s. Increasing numbers of women as well as men pressed for equal rights and an end to discrimination against women. Consistently, women were paid less than men for doing the same job. Many people wanted to end discrimination by adding an amendment called the Equal Rights Amendment (ERA) to the U.S. Constitution. Controversy about the ERA lasted the entire decade and beyond, as many tried (and failed) to make the ERA the law of the land.

The women's liberation movement reached a high water mark in the 1970s. Journalist Gloria Steinem and several other women founded a new magazine, *Ms.,* which began publication in 1972. Feminists explored many aspects of existing American culture, including the roles of women in society and the use of language. For example, English differentiates between the unmarried "Miss" and married "Mrs." A new word was developed as part of nonsexist language, which uses "Ms." to

Bella Abzug was a pioneering feminist. When she graduated from Columbia Law School in 1947, she was one of only a handful of women in the United States who became lawyers that year. She ran for one of New York's two U.S. Senate seats in 1976 but lost in the Democratic primary. *(Lyndon Baines Johnson Presidential Library and Museum)*

Congresswoman Martha Griffiths was the first woman on the powerful Ways and Means committee, and one of the few women in Congress in 1970, which made her influence there all the more remarkable. *(Library of Congress)*

"We were taking back our freedom one foot at a time, one community at a time, one reservation at a time, and it was going to start right now."

—Russell Means, on the AIM occupation of Wounded Knee

refer to both married and unmarried women, just as "Mr." refers to both married and unmarried men.

During the 1970s, many types of jobs became available to women for the first time. More women were elected to serve in Congress. In 1970, two women were appointed as U.S. Army generals. In 1971, the first woman was ordained as an Episcopal priest. In 1972, the FBI hired its first two female agents.

As women pressed for better educational opportunities, the prestigious Ivy League colleges, such as Princeton and Yale, finally began to admit women as students. During the 1970s there was a 500 percent increase in the number of women entering law schools. Forty percent of those entering medical school were women.

THE AMERICAN INDIAN MOVEMENT

Founded by members of the Ojibwa (Annishinabe) Nation, in Minneapolis, Minnesota, in 1969, the American Indian Movement (AIM) was originally dedicated to helping residents of the post–World War II American Indian urban ghettoes deal with discrimination in jobs and housing and with police harassment. The group quickly expanded into a pan–American Indian organization at the center of a new Red Power movement. The growing sense of American Indian pride, fiery speeches, and confrontations with authority at the center of the movement were like those of the Black Panther Party and Black Power philosophy. Dennis Banks, an Ojibwa, and Russell Means, a Lakota, quickly emerged as AIM's most outspoken leaders as local chapters sprung up in cities around the country and eventually on some rural reservations as well.

AIM soon took center stage in some of the most dramatic Indian civil rights protests of the era. In November 1972, AIM members were part of the Trail of Broken Treaties, a series of protest marches on Washington, D.C., that highlighted historical grievances and demanded corrective action from the government. Originally planned as a peaceful civil rights demonstration, the incident turned ugly when negotiations with federal officials broke down, and AIM stepped to the forefront as the situation developed into a siege of the Bureau of Indian Affairs building that lasted for several days.

The following February, AIM members went to the Pine Ridge Reservation in South Dakota to support local Indians who were attempting to impeach the tribal president, Dick Wilson, who was suspected of corruption. When the impeachment failed, local protests continued. Frustrated, the protestors eventually took control of the nearby small town of Wounded Knee, the site of an 1890 massacre of some 300 Indians by the U.S. cavalry. Though AIM was only a small part of the original conflict, they assumed the spotlight as U.S. marshals sealed off the perimeter, initiating a 71-day siege. The event transformed from a local political protest over Indian government into an AIM-run occupation that garnered international press coverage.

A poster calls attention to the Trail of Broken Treaties protest, which was intended to make Americans aware of how the U.S. government had historically ignored its obligations and promises spelled out in treaties with American Indian nations and tribes. (*Michigan State University Library, Special Collections*)

NIXON AND THE ECONOMY

Generally, political conservatives oppose government control of economic programs. Although he considered himself a conservative, in many ways President Nixon was liberal in his economic policies. He accepted federal government economic controls and encouraged direct federal activity in the economy.

Nixon believed in government aid to low-income families. His administration helped to build more public housing units than any before or since. Although he had campaigned against welfare, Nixon offered the

PUBLIC HEALTH CIGARETTE SMOKING ACT

On January 1, 1971, the Public Health Cigarette Smoking Act went into effect, outlawing cigarette advertising on television and radio. It also required a package warning label reading: "Warning: The Surgeon General Has Determined that Cigarette Smoking Is Dangerous to Your Health."

U.S. astronauts explored the moon's surface during NASA's 1971 *Apollo 14* and *Apollo 15* missions.

Apollo spacecraft consisted of two parts: a lunar module that landed and remained on the moon, housing two astronauts, and a command module that orbited the Moon, piloted by another astronaut who picked up the astronauts in the lunar module and then returned to Earth. Several lunar modules remained on the Moon's surface after the Apollo missions ended. (NASA)

Family Assistance Plan, which would have provided a minimum amount of money, food stamps, and subsidies to every American family. This plan proved to be too liberal for conservatives in Congress and too conservative for their liberal colleagues. The bill died in the Senate. One of Nixon's farthest reaching social achievements was his expansion of the Food Stamp Program. By the end of the decade, it was helping to feed 1 in 10 Americans.

SCIENCE

Science in the early 1970s was marked by the signs of things to come in computers. There were no personal computers, but engineers, students, scientists and businesspeople were excited by the newest technology: the small, powerful personal calculator. From 1970 to 1973, several companies, including Texas Instruments, Casio, Commodore, and Hewlett-Packard, introduced a wide variety of hand-held calculators at affordable prices, changing the way people learned and did math forever. Casio put the Pocket Mini on the market in

August 1972, and by the end of 1973, 10 million Casio Minis had been sold.

NASA marked the successful fruition of the Apollo program, which continued to focus on manned exploration of the Moon's surface until its end in 1972. Twice a year, in 1971 and 1972, an Apollo mission landed men on the moon (there were no women astronauts at the time) and returned them safely to earth. The astronauts were scientists who performed experiments dealing with seismic (earthquake) activity, magnetic fields, and meteroids. They brought back almost 800 pounds of moon rock and soil for study.

THE PENTAGON PAPERS

In 1971, *The New York Times* started publishing the defense department's top-secret study of the growth of U.S. military involvement in Vietnam. These documents were called the Pentagon Papers. When they learned what the newspaper was doing, the Department of Justice asked for a temporary restraining order, which was granted.   In its petition to the court, the executive branch of the government asserted that publishing the Pentagon Papers could be a threat to national security. The newspaper countered that not publishing them would violate First Amendment press freedoms provided for under the U.S. Constitution. It also argued that the real government motive was political censorship, rather than protection of national security.

On June 30, the Supreme Court, in *New York Times v. the United States,* ruled in favor of the *Times,* and the documents were published. The Pentagon Papers revealed, among other things, that the government had planned to go into Vietnam even when President Lyndon Johnson was publicly promising not to and that there was no plan to end the war. The publication of the Pentagon Papers helped fuel the debate over the wisdom of U.S. involvement in Vietnam. Most

> **T**echnological advances of the early 1970s included IBM's introduction, in 1970, of the small, portable floppy disk for storage of computer files, and the computer on a chip, or microprocessor, introduced by Intel in 1971.

FASHION AS REBELLION: HOT PANTS

Hot pants were to the early 1970s what the miniskirt was to the 1960s. These tight, abbreviated shorts were very popular among many young women, but they were frowned upon in the workplace. There were restaurants that even prohibited entrance to patrons wearing them. Some businesses took advantage of the fad: Allegheny Airlines even made them a part of the company uniform.

The World Trade Center, also known as the Twin Towers, was completed in 1973. Located at the southern tip of Manhattan, New York City, they were the tallest skyscrapers in the world when they opened. *(NOAA)*

In New York City, one tower of the World Trade Center first opened to the public in 1970, though the upper stories were not completed until 1972. The second tower was completed in 1973.

observers and historians now agree that the publication of the papers did not do injury to the national security of the United States.

The government went on to charge Daniel Ellsberg, the former government employee who made the Pentagon Papers available to the *New York Times,* and his adviser Anthony J. Russo on charges of espionage, theft, and conspiracy. On May 11, 1973, a federal court judge dismissed all charges against them because of improper government conduct.

CHAPTER 2

DARKNESS DESCENDS ON THE WHITE HOUSE, 1972–1974

President Nixon addresses the crowd at his inauguration after winning a landslide victory in his bid for reelection. *(Library of Congress)*

REPUBLICAN CANDIDATE RICHARD Nixon won his second term as U.S. president by a landslide. However, the campaign itself was not without fierce competition, violence, drama, and an interesting cast of American political characters.

Among the Democratic candidates for the nomination was George Wallace, governor of Alabama. During the early 1960s and in Wallace's first run for president in 1968, America had gotten to know all about Wallace as one America's most outspoken supporters of racial segregation. As governor of Alabama, Wallace actively fought against integration, once even standing in the doorway of the University of Alabama to block two

Shirley Chisholm was elected to the House of Representatives in 1968, representing Brooklyn's 12th Congressional District. In 1972, her bid for the Democratic presidential nomination garnered 151 delegate votes. *(Library of Congress)*

"In the end antiblack, antifemale, and all forms of discrimination are equivalent to the same thing — antihumanism."

—Shirley Chisholm, candidate for the 1972 Democratic Party presidential nomination

African-American students from enrolling there. During a rally in May 1972, a man named Arthur Bremer shot Governor Wallace. Wallace was paralyzed from the waist down. Bremer was convicted of attempted murder and sentenced to 53 years in prison.

In contrast to segregationist candidate Wallace, there was Shirley Chisholm, a Congressional representative from Brooklyn, New York. Like Wallace, she was a Democrat. During the 1972 campaign, she became the country's first woman, specifically the first African-American woman, to seek a major political party's nomination for president. Although she did not win the Democratic nomination, she garnered many delegates' votes. She continued to serve in the House of Representatives until 1982.

Other Democratic candidates for the nomination in 1972 included New York City mayor John Lindsay, former presidential nominee Hubert Humphrey, right-leaning Senator Henry (Scoop) Jackson of Washington, left-leaning populist Senator Fred Harris of Oklahoma, South Dakota senator George McGovern, and the front-runner, and moderate Senator Edmund Muskie of Maine.

When Muskie did worse than expected in the New Hampshire primary, McGovern's campaign gained momentum. Muskie was also hurt when he responded emotionally to a negative article about his wife in a conservative newspaper. He was seen on the news apparently in tears, though he later claimed these were melting snowflakes. Nonetheless, the controversy caused public perception of his abilities to erode, and he began to slip in the polls.

McGovern ran a grass-roots campaign centered on social issues, such as ratifying the Equal Rights Amendment and on ending U.S. military involvement in the war in Vietnam. McGovern went on to win the 1972 presidential nomination but lost to President Nixon in a landslide in November's general election. Nixon carried

Governor George Wallace stands in front of a door, attempting to block the integration of the University of Alabama. *(Library of Congress)*

49 states and swept more than 60 percent of the popular vote by running a campaign that painted McGovern as an ultra-liberal who was out of step with the majority of Americans.

THE TROOPS COME HOME

As the 1970s progressed, demonstrations against the Vietnam War became commonplace in the United States. On April 24, 1971 an estimated 500,000 people marched in Washington, D.C., in opposition to the war, and smaller protests occurred weekly at colleges and universities around the nation. Numerous veterans groups began taking part in the antiwar movement. One such group was the Vietnam Veterans Against the War, founded by John Kerry. Participation by veterans groups helped to strengthen the antiwar feeling. Finally, the U.S. government saw that remaining at war in Vietnam was in a no-win situation and began making plans to withdraw its troops.

Under a policy known as "Vietnamization," President Nixon began a slow withdrawal of U.S. troops from Vietnam and sought to transfer the responsibilities of combat to the South Vietnamese army. Though Vietnamization resulted in less U.S. troops seeing combat, the U.S. government continued to bomb the enemy

"If this war mushrooms into a major conflict and a hundred thousand young Americans are killed, it won't be U.S. senators who die. It will be American soldiers who are too young to qualify for the Senate."

—George McGovern, former U.S. Senator and presidential candidate, 1972

McGovern's grass-roots campaign attracted many young people. This T-shirt demonstrates the informal style of the pro-McGovern forces. *(Sarah Parvis)*

Henry Kissinger, secretary of State under Nixon and Ford, orchestrated much U.S. policy in southeast Asia, earning him the enmity of many antiwar protestors. *(Library of Congress)*

In an act of friendship, Communist China gave two giant pandas to the National Zoo in Washington, D.C., in 1972.

from the air, many troops remained in Vietnam, and the process of disengagement was a slow one.

After the establishment of a ceasefire on January 27, 1973, U.S. soldiers began leaving Vietnam for good, ending the longest war in U.S. history. The individuals who negotiated the ceasefire—Nixon's secretary of state Henry A. Kissinger and Le Duc Tho, special adviser to the North Vietnamese delegation to the Paris Peace Talks—were selected for the 1973 Nobel Peace Prize. Mr. Tho declined the honor.

OPENING THE DOOR TO CHINA

Even as the Vietnam War continued with the U.S. military supporting anticommunist South Vietnam, Nixon sought to improve relations between the U.S. and the Communist government of the People's Republic of China. At the time Nixon took office, there was no trade, dialogue, or freedom of travel between the two countries. To many this seemed a stunning contradiction: Nixon was a lifelong anticommunist. He had even been described as paranoid about the Communist threat to the United States. China's Chairman Mao Zedong, fearful of the Soviet Union's aggression, decided he wanted better relations with the United States. Nixon wanted to limit Soviet power and end the Vietnam War. Opening relations with China was a means to an end.

Nixon made the trip to China in February 1972. Until Nixon's visit, there had been no formal diplomatic relations with mainland China since that country's civil war. The war had ended when the Communists, led by Chairman Mao, took over the country in 1949. China's previous rulers, the Nationalists, established a government on the Chinese island province of Taiwan and maintained relations with the United States following the 1949 revolution.

Opening the door to China was possibly Nixon's greatest foreign policy achievement. In his memoirs,

THE McGOVERN CAMPAIGN

After winning the Democratic nomination for president in 1972, George McGovern set out to balance the ticket by finding a suitable person to run for vice president. A number of candidates, including Senator Ted Kennedy of Massachusetts, Governor Pat Lucey of Wisconsin, and Boston mayor Kevin White, either declined or were deemed unsuitable. McGovern finally selected Missouri senator Thomas Eagleton as his running mate. When the media reported that Eagleton had been hospitalized for depression and received electroshock therapy, McGovern initially said that he stood by his choice "one thousand percent." A firestorm soon erupted in the press, however, and Eagleton was asked to leave the ticket. He was replaced by Sargent Shriver, a former ambassador and director of the Peace Corps and brother-in-law of John F. Kennedy.

In another episode occurring shortly after his nomination, McGovern encouraged his campaign adviser Pierre Salinger to meet with the North Vietnamese in Paris. As these talks broke down and word was leaked to the press, another controversy brewed. On Salinger's return, the senator completely disavowed that Salinger had been representing him. Both of these incidents affected McGovern's credibility with the public and caused voters to prefer Nixon.

Nixon recalls standing at the doorway of the presidential jet, *Air Force One*, after it arrived in Beijing, the Chinese capital. He saw Chinese premier Zhou Enlai standing hatless in the cold waiting to greet him. Nixon remembered that the Chinese premier had been deeply offended when, in 1954, Secretary of State John Foster Dulles refused to shake his hand. So Nixon enthusiastically thrust out his hand as he approached Zhou.

Nixon was received by Chairman Mao Zedong and conducted lengthy negotiations with Zhou Enlai. Nixon's choice to visit to China first, instead of the Soviet Union, which had also extended an invitation to the U.S. president, unsettled the Soviets. Though formal diplomatic relations with China were not restored until 1979, the visit opened new possibilities for trade and created semiformal channels of communication between the United States and China. This new era in Chinese-American relations reduced tensions and altered world politics.

President Nixon (right) shakes hands with Chairman Mao, the Communist leader of China. No U.S. president had ever visited China while in office before Nixon. *(National Archives)*

TALKS WITH THE SOVIET UNION

In 1969 the United States and the Communist Soviet Union opened historic talks on the limitation of military

Reclusive American chess phenomenon Bobby Fisher beat the well-known Russian champion, Boris Spassky, for the 1972 world chess title. Taking place with the cold war still an issue, the match could not avoid political implications.

weaponry and strategic arms such as intercontinental ballistic missiles. The Strategic Arms Limitation Talks (SALT) were completed while Nixon visited Moscow in May 1972. This was an important breakthrough in the nuclear arms race because the talks put limits on the numbers of long-range nuclear missiles and defensive missiles each nation could have.

During his stay in the Soviet Union, President Nixon addressed the Russian people on television. In 1973, Soviet Communist party leader Leonid Brezhnev visited the United States. He and Nixon signed a nuclear nonaggression pact and several agreements in science, transportation, and culture.

ROE v. WADE

On January 22, 1973, the U.S. Supreme Court announced one of the most important and controversial decisions of the 20th century. In *Roe v. Wade,* a challenge was made to a Texas statute that made it a crime to perform an abortion unless a woman's life was at stake. The case had been filed by Jane Roe, a legal pseudonym (fake name) for an unmarried woman who wanted to safely and legally end her pregnancy. Siding with Roe, the court struck down the Texas law. In its ruling, the court recognized that the constitutional right to privacy "is broad enough to encompass a woman's decision whether or not to terminate her pregnancy."

Roe v. Wade has come to be known as the case that legalized abortion nationwide. At the time the decision was handed down, nearly all states outlawed abortion. The only exceptions were to save a woman's life, or for limited reasons such as preserving the woman's health, terminating a pregnancy where the fetus had severe birth defects, or in-

Chief Justice Warren Burger presided over the *Roe v. Wade* decision. *(Library of Congress)*

stances of pregnancies resulting from rape or incest. *Roe v. Wade* rendered these laws unconstitutional, making abortion services safer and more accessible to women throughout the country.

Before the Supreme Court ruling, women had to go through illegal, often dangerous channels if they wanted to terminate a pregnancy. Before *Roe v. Wade* became law, these procedures were frequently performed under unsafe or unsanitary conditions. Women could now openly go to their own doctors rather than risk their health in seeking a "backstreet abortion" from an unlicensed practitioner. The decision also set a legal precedent that affected more than 20 subsequent Supreme Court cases involving restrictions on access to abortion.

The National Institute of Mental Health and the U.S. Surgeon General issued a report in 1973 claiming that exposure to violence on television fosters aggression in children.

FREE TO BE YOU AND ME

In the 1970s, many cultural values were questioned by the younger generation. Reassessing traditional gender roles and encouraging young children to be free of outdated societal restrictions was a popular theme. For the first time, television shows with educational content, such as *Sesame Street, Zoom,* and *The Electric Company* were produced in an appealing style that proved popular with children.

Free to Be You and Me (1972) was a television special for children produced by the actress Marlo Thomas, which featured skits, songs, and animated sequences and spawned a popular soundtrack album. Besides being entertaining, *Free to Be You and Me* promoted messages of peaceful co-existence, acceptance of others, and gender equality. Celebrities such as actor Mel Books and football player Rosie Grier appeared on the show singing songs like "When We Grow Up," "It's Alright to Cry," and "Parents Are People" that discouraged gender-based stereotypes.

Three young African-American women gather on a college campus. Their afro hairstyles were very popular in the 1970s, which saw more positive acceptance of different ethnic groups and styles throughout society. *(Sarah Parvis)*

GLORIA STEINEM PUBLISHES *MS.* MAGAZINE

In the early 1970s, Gloria Steinem emerged as a leading figure in the budding women's movement. Her experience in the publishing business, fueled by her political views, convinced her a feminist magazine could be profitable and effective. The first issue of *Ms.* was published in 1972. *Ms.* magazine became an icon in the women's movement, while Gloria Steinem became one of the most recognized American feminists in the world.

The feminist movement of the 1970s also encouraged women to take a more active role in their own health and well being. *Our Bodies, Ourselves,* published by the Boston Women's Health Collective in 1970, was a popular and comprehensive guide to health and sexuality that spoke to women in a clear and open manner that had not been common previously.

Feminist leader Gloria Steinem graduated from Smith College and worked as a Playboy bunny for a journalism assignment before publishing *Ms.* magazine. *(Library of Congress)*

DEATH AT THE OLYMPICS

War and peace in the Middle East were major issues of the 1970s. In 1972, the world got a taste of the terror that those in the Middle East endured on a daily basis.

On September 5, 1972, there were six days left in the Olympic Games, which were being held in Munich, Germany. Eight Arab commandos slipped into the Olympic Village where all the athletes were staying. They killed two Israeli team members and held nine others hostage. Early the next morning, all nine Israelis were killed in a shootout between the terrorists and West German police at a military airport.

Protestors call for the suspension of the Munich Olympics, due to the kidnapping and death of nine Israeli athletes by terrorists. *(AP/Wide World)*

The tragedy stunned the world and stopped the 20th Olympiad in its tracks. But after suspending competition for 24 hours and holding a memorial service attended by 80,000 at the main stadium, the International Olympic Committee ordered that "the Games must go on."

They went on without 22-year-old American swimmer Mark Spitz, who had set an Olympic gold medal record by winning four individual and three relay events, all in world record times. Spitz, an American Jew, was an inviting target for further terrorism and agreed with West German officials when they advised him to leave the country.

SPORTS IN THE SPOTLIGHT

As the 1970s progressed, increased television coverage and the rise of flashy personalities in the world of sports combined to make athletic figures more prominent than ever. The Oakland A's, with their brash green and gold uniforms, long hair, moustaches, and sideburns, reflected the fashion of the times.

With a flamboyant style of play and such stars as Catfish Hunter, Reggie Jackson, and Vida Blue, the A's took the World Series from the Cincinnati Reds in 1972. The press dubbed it a matchup of the Hairs vs. the Squares, so-called because Cincinnati played a more conservative brand of baseball, wore traditional uniforms, and forbade facial hair.

In 1973, Oakland faced the upstart New York Mets. The Mets were underdogs who had been in last place on August 5, $11\frac{1}{2}$ games behind, before rallying down the stretch and winning both their division and the National League pennant in September. Despite Mets manager Yogi Berra's observation that "It ain't over till it's over," the A's triumphed in seven games, and were champs again in 1974, defeating the Los Angeles Dodgers.

> The Oakland A's brought a flashy, modern sensibility to the game and won three consecutive World Series (1972–1974).

"You Gotta Believe!"

—New York Mets pitcher Tug McGraw, coining a phrase that became a rallying cry as the team crawled from last place to capture the 1973 NL pennant

Golda Meir was prime minister of Israel from 1969 to 1974. Born in Kiev, Russia, she emigrated to the United States with her family to escape persecution, and later helped found the state of Israel. Her leadership during the Yom Kippur War earned her both praise and criticism. *(Library of Congress)*

The Sears Tower, second tallest building in the United States, opened in Chicago, Illinois, in 1972.

YOM KIPPUR WAR

On October 6, 1973, Egypt and Syria launched a surprise attack on the Sinai and the Golan Heights, areas held by Israel since the 1967 Six Day War. They were aided both financially and militarily by the governments of Saudi Arabia, Iraq, Kuwait, Libya, Algeria, Morocco, Sudan, Lebanon, and Jordan, The attack came on Yom Kippur, the Jewish Day of Atonement, the holiest day of the Jewish calendar, when Jews spend the day in prayer and do not work, eat, or drink. The assault was also surprising because October 6 fell in the middle of Ramadan, a holy month for Muslims during which they do not take food or drink between sunrise and sunset.

The war lasted for three weeks until Israel was able to repel the Arab armies and push them back beyond the original frontlines. With the confrontation escalating, diplomatic pressure to end the fighting increased. Eventually Israel gained the upper hand, and the oil-producing Arab states imposed an embargo on oil exports to the United States, Israel's strongest supporter. With Israeli troops poised to march on the Arab capitals of Cairo and Damascus, and the Soviet Union threatening direct intervention on behalf of the Arab armies, a ceasefire was implemented on October 22. The war and its outcome represent a turning point in Middle Eastern history. For the first time, vulnerability on the Israeli side was evident, while Syria and Egypt proved their new strength, both militarily and organizationally. The ceasefire did not, however, end the sporadic clashes along the ceasefire lines nor did it dissipate military tensions.

OPEC OIL EMBARGO

In response to President Nixon's giving $2 billion in aid to Israel during the Yom Kippur War, the Arab oil-producing states instituted an embargo (an order by a government prohibiting the departure of commercial ships from its ports) against the United States and other countries that had offered help to Israel. This embargo caused the cost of oil exported to the United States and its European allies to rise by 70 percent. Announced at a meeting of the Organization of Petroleum Exporting Countries (OPEC), the embargo was aimed at countries that supported Israel during the Yom Kippur War. Western Europe imported 80 percent of its oil from the Middle East and was badly affected. The United States imported only about 12 percent of its oil from the Middle East, but it was still seriously affected. In the United States, high oil and gas prices and long lines at gas stations were a common sight, as motorists sometimes lined up for hours to fill their gas tanks. People were forced to car pool, or share rides, to get to work. The American Automobile Association (AAA) reported that 20 percent of the nation's gas stations had no fuel for sale during the final week of February 1974. Gas rationing became commonplace.

The oil embargo was lifted in March 1974 after intense negotiation. However, with the situation in the Middle East continuing to be unstable and Americans driving bigger cars and using more oil than ever, the nation's fuel and energy problems continued.

During the OPEC oil embargo, the U.S. government considered enforcing a strict system of gas rationing like that used during World War II. These gas ration stamps were printed but never issued or used. *(Library of Congress)*

BATTLE OF THE SEXES

In 1973, Billy Jean King was perhaps the best-known female athlete in the world. Not only had she won 16 Wimbledon tennis singles and doubles titles, she was campaigning for gender equity in sports at the height of the women's movement, also known as women's lib. King and others were outraged that women were paid much more poorly than men. For example, when she

Billie Jean King and Bobby Riggs smile during a news conference in New York to publicize their upcoming match at the Houston Astrodome, July 11, 1973. *(AP/Wide World)*

BOBBY RIGGS: MALE CHAUVINIST PIG

Before being defeated by Billie Jean King, Bobby Riggs had defeated a former women's tennis champion, Margaret Court, on May 13, 1973. These matches landed Riggs on the cover of several national magazines. He became an outspoken and somewhat comedic character, hamming it up in print and on television as a so-called *male chauvinist pig*, a term used in the 1970s to describe men opposed to women's equality. Riggs's antics were offensive to some, humorous to others, but most can agree that his showmanship and competitions with Court and King did much to increase the popularity of tennis, and women's tennis in particular.

won the U.S. Open Tennis Championship in 1972, King's prize was $10,000 while the men's champion, Ilie Nastase, won $25,000.

Bobby Riggs, a retired professional tennis player in his 50s, challenged King, who was 29, to a tennis match. He boasted that he would be able to beat her simply because he was a man. "I want Billie Jean King. . . . I want the women's lib leader!" he said. His challenge attracted a lot of media attention; King accepted. The match came to be called The Battle of the Sexes.

The match was held at the Houston Astrodome on September 20, 1973. It got prime time TV coverage and attracted an estimated 40 million viewers. Riggs engaged the crowd by entering the stadium in a carriage pulled by women. Billie Jean King rode in on a red velvet litter carried by University of Houston football players in short togas. However, when they hit the court, Riggs was no match for King, who easily defeated him.

King went on to help organize the Women's Tennis Association, a union of women players that improved their bargaining positions, in 1975. She was the Associated Press's Woman Athlete of the Year in both 1967 and 1973. She was *Sports Illustrated's* Sportswoman of the Year in 1972 and *Time* magazine's Woman of the Year in 1976.

A SLOWING ECONOMY

During the 1970s, the U.S. economy started to experience a number of problems. The oil embargo of 1973–1974 led to high prices for gasoline, and coupled with the United States's dependence on oil for most forms of power, heat and electricity, resulted in what came to be known as the energy crisis. The value of U.S. dollar fell sharply in comparison to foreign currencies around the world in the early 1970s.

In addition, the country was faced with rising unemployment. Many mid-sized cities in the northern and midwestern parts of the country (an area known as the "rust belt,") faced the closing of mills and factories, and the loss of a healthy economic base. Many people who could afford to leave these cities did so, and often times the result was a poverty-stricken, decaying inner-city ringed with middleclass and prosperous suburbs.

BACKLASH AGAINST CIVIL RIGHTS

By the late 1960s, civil rights and government anti-poverty program gains had had positive effects: The African-American middle class grew, and African-American unemployment shrank to under 7 percent in 1968 and 1969. However, during the early 1970s, rising inflation and an economic downturn caused widespread economic uncertainty among African Americans. To deal with difficult issues, a new generation of African-American leaders established new organizations. In 1971, Jesse Jackson founded Operation PUSH (People United to Save Humanity) in Chicago to work for the economic advancement of poor people.

The struggling economy fueled white opposition to government programs that benefited African Americans. The policy of affirmative action, which provided preferential treatment in education and employment opportunities to minorities who had been previously discriminated against, was seen as reverse racism by

Pong, the first video game, was invented in 1972. The game featured primitive graphics meant to simulate a game of table tennis, and proved so popular that the home version, for use with television sets, sold in huge numbers when it was released in 1975.

Jesse Jackson (center) emerged as a leader of the African-American community. He led several protests seeking increased job opportunities for African Americans. *(Library of Congress)*

some. School busing, or transporting students outside of their communities to achieve school integration, was a controversial measure enacted in the 1970s that caused some whites to feel that African Americans were benefiting at their expense. White protestors burned buses, harassed African-American schoolchildren, and supported local politicians who opposed African-American equality. A surprising number of northern voters supported the presidential candidacy of segregationist George Wallace in both 1968 and 1972.

EQUAL EMPLOYMENT/ EQUAL OPPORTUNITY

The Equal Employment Opportunity Act of 1972 made it illegal to discriminate against employees or potential employees because of race, color, religion, sex, or national origin. This was an extension of the provision of the Civil Rights Act of 1964, which was intended to ensure that discrimination would not occur in voting rights, accommodations, public facilities, federal assistance, education, or health care.

In 1972, it was added to the Civil Rights Act that there should be no intention "to discriminate because of race, color, religion, sex, or national origin." During the next year, Congress passed the the Rehabilitation Act of 1973, which made it illegal to discriminate against people with disabilities in the federal government.

THE WATERGATE SCANDAL

The ongoing conflict over U.S. involvement in Vietnam remained a volatile issue throughout the 1972 presidential campaign. Despite this, Nixon ran for re-election and soundly defeated George McGovern. Toward the end of the campaign a group of burglars broke into the Democratic Party campaign headquarters in Washington's Watergate hotel and office complex, affixing wiretaps in the office to eavesdrop on the campaign workers. Two reporters for a local newspaper, The *Washington Post*, first broke the story, and as the involvement of high ranking government officials began to surface, the incident became national news. The reporters, Bob Woodward and Carl Bernstein, were fed tips from a mysterious informant they called Deep Throat. (More than 30 years later in June 2005, Deep Throat revealed himself to be

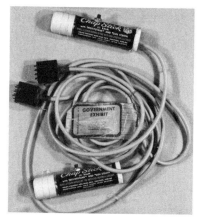

These ChapStick tubes contained tiny microphones; they are a bug, or secret listening device. These were to be planted by Republican operatives in the Democratic campaign offices at the Watergate hotel. *(National Archives)*

Nixon sits in an informal meeting with several of the co-conspirators in the Watergate scandal. *(Nixon Presidential Library)*

"...all [Nixon] can show us, after five years of total freedom to do anything he wants with all this power, is a shattered national economy, disastrous defeat in a war we could have ended four years ago on far better terms than he finally came around to, and a hand-picked personal staff...whose collective criminal record will blow the minds of high-school American History students for the next 100 years."

—"Gonzo" Journalist Hunter S. Thompson, excerpt from an essay in *Rolling Stone* magazine, September 1973

Mark Felt, a former number two official at the FBI). Woodward and Bernstein won many major journalism awards for investigative reporting, including the Pulitzer Prize. They wrote two books about their experience during the Watergate investigation: *All the President's Men* and *The Final Days.*

The Nixon administration denied knowledge of the break-in. However, it soon became clear that administration officials had tried to cover up the burglary and any connections to it. The break-in was tied to a fundraising organization for the Nixon campaign known popularly as CREEP (Committee to Re-elect the President), headed by Nixon operative G. Gordon Liddy, under the auspices of U.S. attorney general John Mitchell. Later investigations would link the Watergate break-in and cover up to high-ranking officials in the Nixon administration, including White House counsel John Dean, John Ehrlichman, the assistant to the president for domestic affairs, and Nixon's chief of staff H. R. Haldeman. Under congressional and public pressure, Nixon appointed a special prosecutor. When the special prosecutor learned that the president had secretly taped conversations in the Oval Office, he filed a subpoena to secure tapes he believed relevant to the criminal investigation.

The president and his chief assistants denied involvement, but as evidence that the White House was involved in the break-in and cover-up continued to grow, the U.S. Congress was compelled to investigate what role the Watergate matter might have played in undermining, or attempting to undermine, the 1972 election process. The Senate Select Committee on Presidential Campaign Activities began public hearings on May 17, 1973. These came be known as the Watergate hearings.

Television cameras covered the Watergate hearings in their entirety, from the first day until they ended in August 1973. Americans were riveted to their television screens, watching the drama unfold. At the time massive television coverage of this sort was uncommon. Never before had the intimate workings of the U.S. government been on public display like this. The networks amassed 319 hours of footage, a record at the time for coverage of a single event.

THREATENED WITH IMPEACHMENT, NIXON RESIGNS

In March 1974, a federal grand jury indicted seven associates of President Nixon for conspiracy to obstruct justice and other offenses relating to the Watergate burglary. The president himself was named as a co-conspirator, but he was not indicted. The district court issued a subpoena, a legal document commanding the president to testify in court and requiring him to produce certain tapes and papers relating to precisely identified meetings between himself and others. Nixon refused to turn these tapes over on grounds of "executive privilege," a legal claim that allows the executive

"People have got to know whether or not their president is a crook. Well, I am not a crook."

—Nixon to a convention of editors, Orlando, Florida, November 17, 1973

A PRESIDENT RESIGNS

. . . I have concluded that because of the Watergate matter I might not have the support of the Congress that I would consider necessary to back the very difficult decisions and carry out the duties of this office in the way the interests of the Nation would require.

I have never been a quitter. To leave office before my term is completed is abhorrent to every instinct in my body. But as President, I must put the interest of America first. America needs a full-time President and a full-time Congress, particularly at this time with problems we face at home and abroad.

To continue to fight through the months ahead for my personal vindication would almost totally absorb the time and attention of both the President and the Congress in a period when our entire focus should be on the great issues of peace abroad and prosperity without inflation at home.

Therefore, I shall resign the Presidency effective at noon tomorrow. Vice President Ford will be sworn in as President at that hour in this office.

Farewell. Always give your best. Never get discouraged. Never be petty. Always remember: Others may hate you. Those who hate you don't win unless you hate them. And then you destroy yourself.

—Nixon, farewell speech to the White House staff, August 9, 1974

Richard and Pat Nixon say good-bye to President Gerald and First Lady Betty Ford as the Nixons leave the White House for the last time. *(Nixon Presidential Library)*

branch of government to justify withholding of documents and information from other branches of government. Chief Justice Burger reaffirmed the ruling that under the Constitution the courts have the final voice in determining constitutional questions. This means that not even the president of the United States is above the law.

On August 5, 1974, transcripts of 64 tape recordings were released, including one that was particularly damaging. This became known as the so-called smoking gun tape when it revealed that Nixon had participated in the Watergate cover-up as far back as June 23, 1972. Nixon had suggested paying the Watergate burglars to keep them from talking, ordered illegal wiretaps, used campaign funds illegally (such as to illegally finance travel for White House aides), and directed the FBI to stop their investigation.

Never before has a U.S. president been so exposed to public scrutiny. The tapes not only laid bare evidence of wrongdoing with regard to Watergate but also revealed unflattering aspects of Nixon's personality, such as tendencies toward vindictiveness and bigotry. This was the final blow to the Nixon presidency. The president was facing the prospect of impeachment hearings, and around the country there were calls for him to resign. Three days later, on August 8, with his support in Congress almost completely gone, Nixon announced that he would resign. Nineteen White House aides and associates would eventually serve prison terms.

1972–74: THREE YEARS, THREE VICE PRESIDENTS

The early 1970s saw a string of three vice-presidents in rapid succession. The office, usually known for its non-controversial, low-profile occupants, attracted more

After assuming the presidency, Gerald Ford appointed the former governor of New York, Nelson Rockefeller, to be his vice president. Nelson Rockefeller was a political moderate and prominent member of a political dynasty founded by his grandfather, the oil baron John D. Rockefeller.

President Ford testifies before Congress on the Watergate scandal. *(Library of Congress)*

Vice President Spiro T. Agnew gestures on August 8, 1973, at a Washington news conference during which he stated he would not resign. (*AP/Wide World*)

attention than ever during the turmoil of the Watergate and post-Watergate years.

Spiro Agnew came to office as vice president well-known for his forthright attacks on liberals and anti-war activists, as well as his criticism of the media and college professors and intellectuals. He was born in 1918, in Baltimore, Maryland, to a family of Greek immigrants. His last name was originally Anagnostopoulos, and in later years he noted that he had been the victim of ethnic prejudice. After serving in World War II, he went to law school, became a lawyer, and became active in Baltimore and Maryland politics. He was nominated for the vice presidency in 1968 and re-elected in 1972.

He was forced to resign in October 1973 after the Justice Department revealed that there was evidence he had accepted bribes while holding a variety of offices in Maryland. He was accused of federal income tax evasion and rather than face a trial, he pleaded *nolo contendere*, which meant he accepted the court's punishment without pleading either innocent or guilty. He

"A little over a week ago, I took a rather unusual step for a vice president . . . I said something."

—Spiro Agnew, 1971

was disbarred in Maryland, which meant he could no longer practice law, and paid a fine of $10,000. His career ended in disgrace. Agnew was only the second U.S. vice president to resign from office, and the first to do so because of scandal. (John Calhoun had resigned the office in 1832 to take a seat in the Senate.)

In 1973, Gerald Ford became Nixon's next vice president. When Nixon resigned on August 9, 1974, Ford was sworn in as the 38th president of the United States. Ford was the first vice president and the first president to ascend to both positions without being elected.

Ford appointed Nelson Rockefeller to fill the vacant vice presidential position, and the Congress confirmed him after a prolonged series of hearings. Many Congressmen expressed concern about his great personal wealth.

Born in 1908 as a grandson of John D. Rockefeller, the founder of Standard Oil, young Nelson had a privileged upbringing that nonetheless stressed the

At the 1972 Republican convention, Convention Chairman Gerald Ford introduces New York State governor Nelson Rockefeller. Less than two years later, the two men would be president and vice president, respectively. (*AP/Wide World*)

importance of public service. He served in the federal government in several appointed positions throughout World War II, then moved into New York State politics. He ran unsuccessfully for the presidency in 1960, 1964, and 1968. His tenure as vice president was uneventful, for the most part, although an incident with a heckler in 1976, in which he used a rude gesture, garnered much media attention. He declined to run for vice president in 1976, and Senator Bob Dole filled that slot instead.

CHAPTER 3

THE 1970s BEGIN AGAIN, 1974–1975

O N AUGUST 9, 1974, FOLLOWING THE resignation of Richard Nixon, Gerald R. Ford was sworn in as the 40th U.S. president. A native of Michigan, Ford was elected to the House of Representatives in 1948 and served for 13 consecutive terms. Ford had a reputation of being a person of honesty and integrity, which was something the country sorely needed after the Watergate scandal.

James Cannon, who worked for President Ford when he was in the White House, put it this way:

President Gerald R. Ford eats breakfast in the White House in 1974. Ford's straightforward, wholesome character was welcomed by many Americans after the Watergate scandal. *(Library of Congress)*

> **A**s journalist John Osborne summarized it, Ford was seen as "a loser, a bumbler, a misfit President who for some reason or other...was prone to slip on airplane ramps, bump his head on helicopter entrances, entangle himself in the leashes of his family dogs, and fall from skis in front of television cameras that showed him asprawl in snow."

Gerald R. Ford became president not because he was popular with the American public, not because he campaigned for the job, but because of his character...Ford personified what Nixon was not. Ford was honest. He could be trusted.

Ford assured the nation when he took office that "our long national nightmare is over" and pledged "openness and candor" in all his actions. He won a warm response from the Democratic 93rd Congress when he said he wanted "a good marriage" rather than a honeymoon with his former colleagues.

NIXON'S BLANKET PARDON

The new president's popularity took a downward turn fairly rapidly when, after one month as president, Ford gave Richard Nixon a blanket pardon on September 9, 1974, that absolved Nixon of any crimes he might

President Ford answers a barrage of questions from reporters on the White House lawn after his unconditional pardon of Richard Nixon. *(Ford Presidential Library)*

have committed while president. This meant that Nixon would not have to face criminal indictment or stand trial for any criminal wrongdoing in which he may have been involved with regard to Watergate or its subsequent cover-up.

Ford announced the pardon in a televised speech to the nation: "After years of bitter controversy and divisive national debate, I have been advised, and I am compelled to conclude that many months and perhaps more years will have to pass before Richard Nixon could obtain a fair trial by jury in any jurisdiction of the United States under governing decisions of the Supreme Court." Essentially, the new president was saying that Nixon would never be able to receive a fair trial for his alleged cover-up of Watergate.

"Finally, I feel that Richard Nixon and his loved ones have suffered enough and will continue to suffer, no matter what I do, no matter what we, as a great and good nation, can do together to make his goal of peace come true," he concluded. Many people felt that the pardon was part of a secret deal between Nixon and Ford, and that Ford had agreed to pardon him if Nixon resigned. Ford denied the accusation, insisting that a long trial would have damaged the country.

While it was clear that Nixon had committed crimes, many Americans expressed the cynical belief that Nixon had done what other presidents before him had done, but he just got caught. Watergate has become such a metaphor for scandal that now the suffix "-gate" gets attached to all kinds of other words: Iran-Contragate, Travelgate, Monicagate. Just suggesting Watergate as a historical marker conveys scandal.

One of the next things Gerald Ford did when he became president was to offer amnesty to Vietnam War draft resisters. According to Ford, he did this in an effort to "heal the country's wounds (and) end the divisiveness." There was a great deal of controversy about Ford's plan, as it came on the heels of his unconditional

President Ford and Secretary of State Henry Kissinger talk outside the White House. *(Library of Congress)*

Top ballet dancer **Mikhail Baryshnikov** defected from the Soviet Union and joined the American Ballet Theatre in New York City in 1974. (At the time, the Soviet Union prevented its citizens from traveling freely and taking jobs in other countries.)

> *"I prefer to consider the reality of America…we have attained a remarkable self-governed society that possesses the flexibility and dynamism to grow and undertake an entirely new agenda—an agenda for America's third century."*
>
> —President Gerald R. Ford,
> April 1975

The telephone answering machine was invented in 1975, as was the first home videotape cassette recorder, Sony's Betamax. In 1976, Matsushita introduced the competing VHS system which eventually captured the market.

ASSASSINATION ATTEMPTS

Twice in September 1975, President Ford was the target of assassination attempts. Both of these attempts were made by women. During the first attempt, in Sacramento, California, on September 5, Secret Service agents intervened, and subdued the gun-wielding woman, Lynette "Squeaky" Fromme, before shots were fired. On September 22, in San Francisco, the would-be assassin, Sara Jane Moore, fired one shot at Ford but missed by several feet.

Secret Service agents race toward Lynette "Squeaky" Fromme. Two women, Fromme and Sara Jane Moore, separately attempted to assassinate President Ford in September 1975. *(Gerald R. Ford library)*

pardon of Nixon. Under Ford's plan, his pardon of draft resisters was conditional. They would have to agree to work at some form of public service or community job for a period of two years. Many war resisters who had left the country did not return until years after the pardon, when the conditions for their re-entry had eased.

FOREIGN POLICY

In foreign policy, Ford and Secretary of State Henry Kissinger continued the policy of reducing tension with the Soviet Union and encouraging a warming of the cold war between the two nations. This policy was called *détente.*

Relations between the United States and the Soviets were characterized by several activities. There were ongoing arms negotiations. The Helsinki Accords, agreed to by the United States, Canada, Western Europe, and the Soviet Union, were a pledge to respect general human rights principles and national boundaries. A joint Apollo-Soyuz joint manned space flight was another symbol of cooperation.

Apollo-Soyuz's space flight became a symbol of progress in the United States's relations with the Soviet Union. A drawing of the American and Soviet spacecrafts depicts them in orbit together. *(NASA)*

CLOSING THE CHAPTER ON VIETNAM

The fighting between North and South Vietnam continued following U.S. withdrawal from the region in 1973. Without support from the United States, the South Vietnamese army began to fall apart by early 1975.

Throughout April 1975, the Communists, known as the Viet Cong, closed in on the South Vietnamese capital of Saigon (today called Ho Chi Minh City).

Prince Norodom Sihanouk desperately tried to preserve Cambodia's neutrality while the Vietnam War raged. His efforts could not prevent the war from entering his country on March 18, 1970. *(Library of Congress)*

"If the Americans do not want to support us anymore, let them go, get out! Let them forget their humanitarian promises!"

—Nguyen Van Thieu, president of South Vietnam, 1975

"Vietnam was what we had instead of happy childhoods."

—Michael Herr, 1977, writer and producer of two films about Vietnam

President Ford ordered an airlift of anticommunist Vietnamese refugees from the city of Da Nang. Most of the refugees were taken to the United States.

The remaining Americans were forced to evacuate Saigon as the city fell to the invading Viet Cong. Emergency helicopters took off from the roof of the U.S. embassy, carrying the evacuees to ships waiting off the coast. Americans at home in the United States watched on television as thousands of South Vietnamese, who feared the Communist takeover, tried to join the Americans during the evacuation of Saigon. There was tearful chaos as South Vietnamese tried to force their way onto helicopters that could barely fly, weighted by all the people hanging on.

After the Viet Cong flag was raised in Saigon, South Vietnam surrendered to the Communists. For the Americans, it signaled the end of not only a long and bloody battle but also a decades-long war. President Ford said the whole ordeal "closes a chapter in the American experience." Finally, on April 30, 1975, the South Vietnamese president surrendered unconditionally to the Communists of North Vietnam.

GENOCIDE IN CAMBODIA

Parallel to the fall of South Vietnam to the Viet Cong, the Communist Party of Cambodia, the nation bordering South Vietnam to the west, staged a military coup and established a new government. The leaders of the Communist Party, which was known as the Khmer Rouge, renamed Cambodia *Democratic Kampuchea.* Within days of the capture of Cambodia's capital, Phnom Penh, the city's entire population of more than 2 million people was marched into the countryside at gunpoint.

Pol Pot, the leader of the Khmer Rouge, declared April 17, 1975, to be the beginning of "Year Zero" and proceeded with a ruthless program to rid Cambodian society of capitalism, Western culture, religion, and all foreign influences. No opposition was tolerated.

Pol Pot's plans were carried out swiftly and severely. Foreigners were expelled, embassies closed, and the currency abolished. Markets, schools, newspapers, religious practice, and private property were outlawed. Members of the previous government, public servants, police, military officers, teachers, ethnic Vietnamese, Christian clergy, Muslims, and members of the educated middle-class were identified and executed.

The ruling Khmer Rouge forced nearly the entire country's population out of the cities and towns and into agricultural collectives, the so-called killing fields. An estimated 1.5 to 3 million men, women, and children died between 1975 and 1979. In December 1978, after several years of border conflict and a flood of Cambodian refugees into Vietnam, Vietnamese troops invaded, capturing Phnom Penh on January 7, 1979, and deposing the Khmer Rouge regime.

A SUFFERING DOMESTIC ECONOMY

Along with the tremendous amount of unrest overseas following the U.S. departure from Vietnam, Americans

"The chopper had its tail ramp up; I threw in a bag, but I couldn't make it. Someone grabbed my arm and I was dragged onboard and across the floor. Seconds later, in a roar, the chopper lifted off."

—Laurie Palmer, reporter and writer, on the evacuation from Saigon as the North Vietnamese took over the city

"FORD TO CITY: DROP DEAD"

So read the front-page headline of New York's *Daily News* on October 30, 1975, after President Ford initially refused to consider giving federal loans to the city of New York, which was then on the brink of financial collapse. Ford never actually uttered the words, and as the larger implications of such an event became clear, Ford retreated from his earlier position. In spite of the controversy, the paper endorsed Ford's presidential bid the next year, but the city's voters did not. New York State's 41 electoral votes went to Jimmy Carter.

President Ford shares a laugh with Speaker of the House Tip O'Neill, a Democrat. Faced with a floundering economy, Ford struggled to pass his proposed tax cuts and other plans in a Democratic-controlled Congress. *(Library of Congress)*

First Lady Betty Ford found that her forthright and open involvement in issues ranging from women's health to addiction caused controversy. *(Library of Congress)*

had many issues to pay attention to at home. Ford had inherited from Nixon the weakest U.S. economy since the beginning of World War II, 30 years earlier. The unemployment rate was high, and Americans began hearing the term *inflation* every day.

During periods of inflation, prices rise. Everything seems to increase in value except money; $1 might buy a loaf of bread in January, but by September, it would take $1.50 to buy that same loaf of bread. Usually, inflation occurs during wartime because consumer goods become scarce while the factories make war supplies, and so people will pay more for the hard-to-find goods. The 1970s was America's only period of serious peacetime inflation.

In October 1974, in response to rising inflation, Ford went on television and spoke to the American people. He asked them to "whip inflation now" (WIN) and urged them to wear WIN buttons. Most people perceived this as a public relations act, rather than a reflection of any real plan to heal the economy.

In 1974, there was a national election for Congress members and senators. The Republican Party suffered substantial losses, due both to Watergate and the sad state of the economy. To deal with the economic recession, Ford proposed tax cuts and other plans. The Democratic-controlled Congress opposed many elements of Ford's program.

Ford proposed heavy taxes on imported oil. However, Congress hindered Ford's attempt to deregulate the price of domestic oil. Ford wanted foreign oil prices to rise, perhaps reducing oil consumption and stimulating domestic production at the same time. With increased domestic production and deregulation of domestic oil prices, Ford and his economists believed the price of domestic oil would drop. However, Ford was unable to convince Congress to deregulate oil prices. Consequently, as oil prices increased, Ford was forced to rely on voluntary measures by U.S. citizens to conserve energy.

BETTY FORD

President Ford's wife, Betty, broke fresh ground for a first lady with her forthrightness on controversial and personal matters. As first lady, Betty Ford continued her work with handicapped children and used her knowledge about women's issues to help others. In fact, she was very involved in speaking out for abortion rights and working for the passage of the Equal Rights Amendment, although the attempt to pass the amendment was ultimately unsuccessful.

Betty Ford was diagnosed with breast cancer in 1974, and by going public about her illness and surgery she became an honest and vocal advocate for increased awareness about this and other women's health issues. During her tenure as first lady she helped millions to understand breast cancer and take personal responsibility for their bodies.

Betty Ford also expressed uncommon understanding for some of the new norms of young people's behavior, including premarital sex and the use of marijuana, and was candid about undergoing treatment for her addictions to prescription drugs and alcohol. She later went on to co-found the Betty Ford Center, a California rehabilitation facility for the treatment of chemical dependency.

FORD'S FAMOUS FUMBLES

Despite a distinguished college football career at the University of Michigan and a reputation as an accomplished athlete, Ford had an undeserved reputation for being extremely clumsy. The media, especially television, often chose to show footage of Ford's missteps on staircases, or of him bumping his head on the doorway of *Air Force One*. This image was popularized by a series of skits on *Saturday Night Live,* NBC's weekly late night live comedy show. Cast member Chevy Chase portrayed Ford as a man who was literally incapable of taking a single step

LEONARD PELTIER

After the occupation of Wounded Knee, AIM went into decline. Though its leaders Banks and Means escaped serious legal consequences, prominent AIM activist Leonard Peltier was convicted and sentenced to consecutive life sentences for the murder of two FBI agents in 1975. The case has raised serious questions about tampered and fabricated evidence, intimidated witnesses, and federal procedures, so much so that Amnesty International classifies Peltier as a political prisoner. However, his case has received more attention abroad than in the United States, and he was still incarcerated as of late 2005.

The jailing of AIM activist Leonard Peltier was met with numerous protests. *(AP/Wide World)*

MUHAMMAD ALI: "THE GREATEST"

"Float like a butterfly, sting like a bee." This was the catch phrase of Muhammad Ali, dominant heavyweight fighter of the 1970s, who won the world title on three separate occasions. Born Cassius Clay in Louisville, Kentucky, January 17, 1942, he joined the Nation of Islam and changed his name to Muhammad Ali after claiming his first title in 1964. Citing his religious convictions, Ali refused to serve in the U.S. military in Vietnam, a polarizing stance that won him as many detractors as admirers. His title was revoked, and he was sentenced to prison for draft evasion. Ali remained free on appeal, and the conviction was reversed by the U.S. Supreme Court in 1971, but still, he had been unable to box for over three years.

Charismatic, outspoken, and political, Ali was nicknamed "The Greatest," and became an international celebrity known for his humanitarian work, alongside his skill and showmanship. He regained his heavyweight crown in the so-called Rumble in the Jungle against George Foreman, in Kinshasa, Zaire, in October of 1974. His three bouts with Joe Frazier are considered some of the best in boxing history. The telegenic Ali became one of the most popular athletes of his or any era, his interviews with broadcaster Howard Cosell standing out as particularly enlightening and entertaining exchanges. Ali retired from the ring in 1981, and despite battling Parkinson's disease he remained a hero to millions around the globe.

"I am America. I am the part you won't recognize. But get used to me. Black, confident, cocky; my name, not yours; my religion, not yours; my goals, my own; get used to me."

—Heavyweight champion of the world, Muhammad Ali, 1975

ABC, CBS, and NBC agreed to create a family hour, an early evening time slot for shows free of violence and sex.

without falling over or destroying something. Many of Ford's supporters denounced this stereotype as unfair, saying the president was no clumsier than any normal person, but his blunders continued to receive publicity.

SATURDAY NIGHT LIVE

October 11, 1975, saw the debut of a late night television comedy show that was totally different in its scope and attitude than anything that had come previously. The show, broadcast live at 11:30 P.M., was *NBC's Saturday Night*, (later *Saturday Night Live*), and it eventually went on to become one of the most popular shows in television history. *Saturday Night* combined satirical sketches, music, and films and consistently pushed the envelope when it came to broadcasting a new brand of comedy. Produced by Lorne Michaels, the program featured a different host and musical guest each week, and a stable of regular performers known as the Not Ready for Prime Time Players.

The show's attitude was irreverent and questioning of authority, and it struck a strong post-Watergate chord with young audiences who had come of age in the

1960s. *Saturday Night* often dealt with political and sexual themes, incorporating the drug-based humor that was part of a new style of comedy that sprung up in the 1970s. Other examples of this kind of humor could be found in the magazine *National Lampoon* and the comedy routines of Cheech and Chong and Richard Pryor.

Ratings were low at first, and producer Michaels frequently had to fight the network's censors to air many skits. By 1976, however, *Saturday Night Live* had hit its stride. Though the show would occasionally fluctuate in popularity (and humorous content) over the following years, it became a staple of late night television, and cast members like Chevy Chase, Gilda Radner, Dan Aykroyd, and John Belushi would go on to become major stars.

MOVIES

Cinema in the 1970s followed the trend toward more realistic, rougher-edged films and authentic characterizations that had emerged in the 1960s. The invention of the steadicam, in 1970, improved the mobility of film crews, allowing for a wider range of locations for shooting. The work of directors such as Martin Scorsese and Francis Ford Coppola, and performers such as

"Good Evening, I'm Chevy Chase, and you're not."

—Comedian Chevy Chase, host of the Weekend Update segment on NBC's *Saturday Night Live*

John Belushi created memorable characters on *Saturday Night Live* as well as in movies such as *Animal House* and *The Blues Brothers*. Here, he appears in *Continental Divide*. (*AP/Wide World*)

HOWARD COSELL

Born in Brooklyn, New York, in 1920, Howard Cosell was one of the most recognizable faces of the 1970s. With his distinctive, (some would say grating) nasal delivery, Cosell was ubiquitous on television, hosting ABC's "Monday Night Football," major boxing matches, even his own variety show. Though some found him aggravating, and he was sometimes mocked for his unusual, abrasive style, he garnered respect for his unique perspective and intelligent commentary. Before Cosell came along, sports reporting tended toward more lightweight fare.

Cosell's interviews of sports figures were provocative and featured deeper, thoughtful questions that set a new standard in broadcast journalism. His often contentious dialogues with Muhammad Ali were as illuminating as they were hilarious, and despite their differences the two developed admiration for one another. Cosell was among the first to refer to Ali by his Muslim name, and he strongly defended Ali's political stance against the Vietnam War, which generated controversy. Outspoken till the end, Cosell died in 1995 at the age of 77.

STREAKING

The 1970s were full of fads. Some were fun, some were just bad. In spring 1974, on college campuses across the country, the fad of streaking, or running nude in crowded public places, began. Whatever the reasoning, streaking became a part of everyday campus life and eventually spread to other public arenas. Some did it as a political protest. One young man darted through the state legislative chamber of Hawaii proclaiming himself the "Streaker of the House." Other public exhibitionists turned up everywhere from the 1974 Academy Awards to the closing ceremonies of the 1976 Summer Olympics.

Woody Allen made some of the most popular comedies of the 1970s, such as *Sleeper*. (*AP/Wide World*)

SAYING IT IN THE 1970s: A GLOSSARY OF SLANG

bogart To keep for one's self, be greedy

boogie To dance or move quickly

book To go, leave a place, as in "Let's book out of here!"

boss Cool, awesome

bread Money, cash, as in "Can you lend me some bread?"

bum To acquire by begging, as in "Hey dude, can I bum a ride?"

bummer A depressing, negative event or thing. "That movie was a bummer."

dy-no-mite Great, excellent

far out Way cool

foxy Good-looking (male or female)

hang To be in a place or with a person, wait

grass Marijuana

groovy Cool

heavy Serious, weighty, or powerful

jive turkey A detestable person

mellow out Calm down, relax

right on Good; an expression of accepting something

see ya on the flipside See you later.

streak To run in public in the nude. Streaking was very popular in 1974.

Robert De Niro and Jodie Foster continued a movement that veered away from the typical Hollywood depictions of previous generations and explored situations that were of a grimmer and more controversial nature. Other types of movies flourished as well during the decade, such as the witty comedies of Woody Allen, which found a wide audience.

One genre that flourished in the 1970s was the disaster movie. Long before computer-driven animation and CGI effects could create environments where anything could happen on screen, Hollywood producers such as Irwin Allen were crafting disaster-themed epics that did big business at the box office. The elements of a disaster movie were fairly consistent: a large all-star cast, a human-made or natural catastrophe, and much property damage. Classic disaster movies included Allen's *The Poseidon Adventure* (1972), about survivors trying to escape a ship capsized by a tidal wave and *The Towering Inferno* (1974), about a skyscraper on fire, as well as the self-explanatory *Earth-quake* (1974), and *The Hindenburg* (1975), about the 1937 zeppelin explosion.

OTHERWORLDLY SOUNDS

While the early part of the decade saw the success of singer-songwriters such as Cat Stevens and James Taylor, with their relatively humble style of dress and soft sound, by mid-decade a flashier style of showmanship had begun to dominate the pop charts.

The British pianist and singer Elton John gained recognition for his larger-than-life stage persona, incorporating extravagant sets, flamboyant costumes, and a mind-boggling variety of different eyeglasses. John was the biggest selling pop act in America through the middle of the decade, with albums such as *Goodbye Yellow Brick Road* (1973) and *Captain Fantastic and the Brown Dirt Cowboy* (1975) achieving massive record sales. Between 1972 and 1976 John scored sixteen consecutive top-20 hits on the pop charts.

The glam rock movement incorporated similar flash and glitter along with a harder rock sound, as the early 1970s saw the rise in popularity of theatric performers, including Alice Cooper and David Bowie. Underground acts such as Lou Reed and the New York Dolls made a significant cultural impact with their androgynous attire and risqué lyrical content.

The logical progression beyond glam rock culminated with the arrival of the hard rock band KISS into American consciousness in 1974. KISS captured the imagination of an entire generation of bored suburban youth with a carefully projected image of tongue-in-cheek demonic shtick that produced a fervor not seen since the Beatlemania craze of the 1960s. The four-piece band always appeared in full fright make-up, wearing outrageous costumes and honing a stage show that featured smoke, explosions, fire-breathing, blood

AARON BREAKS RUTH'S RECORD

On April 8, 1974, Hank Aaron of the Atlanta Braves hit the 715th home run of his major league career, surpassing Babe Ruth's home run record. Twenty-five years after African Americans were admitted into the major leagues, Aaron still received hate mail from white supremacists as he approached Ruth's record.

Hank Aaron smiles after he tied Babe Ruth's all-time home run record of 714. *(AP/Wide World)*

spitting, and the type of fist-in-the-air heavy metal that captivated young audiences around the country. KISS remained astoundingly popular throughout the rest of the 1970s, galvanizing a devoted fan base known as the Kiss Army, and merchandising everything from posters and comic books, (printed with miniscule amounts of real blood in the ink), to wallpaper and stationery.

Gene Simmons, lead singer of KISS, was never photographed without his elaborate stage makeup, adding to the group's mystique. *(AP/Wide World)*

CHAPTER 4

CARTER COMES TO WASHINGTON, 1976–1977

I N 1976, PRESIDENT FORD RAN FOR RE-election. He was challenged for the Republican nomination by former screen actor and California governor Ronald Reagan, but Ford gained the vote of just enough delegates at the Republican convention to become the Republican candidate. The president selected Kansas senator Robert Dole as his running mate.

Chief Justice Warren E. Burger (sixth from left, center) administers the oath of office to Jimmy Carter on the east portico of the U.S. Capitol on January 20, 1977. *(Library of Congress)*

Jimmy Carter may have been a Washington outsider, but he had a long career in politics in Georgia at the state level.
(Library of Congress)

The Democratic nominee in 1976 was Jimmy Carter. A successful peanut farmer from Plains, Georgia, who had long been active in state politics, Carter had been elected Georgia's governor in 1970. With his vice presidential candidate, Senator Walter Mondale of Minnesota, Carter ran an effective campaign as a reformer and Washington newcomer. Many voters found his outsider status attractive because he was not associated with the Watergate scandal. Even though President Ford was not connected personally to Watergate, voters still associated him with the Nixon administration, especially after Ford had granted Nixon a pardon for Watergate crimes. With the nation suffering from a slow economy, and a widespread desire for change in Washington, Jimmy Carter beat Ford in one of the closest elections in American history.

President Jimmy Carter entered Washington political life as an outsider. People considered him a good potential president because of his personable nature. Carter had served in the U.S. Navy and worked as a farmer, and as a newcomer to the national political stage, he promised the nation a new beginning.

The atmosphere of cynicism and mistrust of government that pervaded American culture during the early 1970s continued during the Ford and Carter years. While much of that is usually attributed to the Watergate scandal, political misdeeds and misdoings had been uncovered during previous decades without causing similar levels of public outrage. Some historians think that Americans' sense of disappointment in their leaders and their government was more directly tied to the Vietnam War and social upheaval of the 1960s.

Jimmy Carter promised to heal the wounds of Watergate and Vietnam and to head a government as good, decent, and compassionate as the American people. In fact, in 1977 he published a book entitled *A Government as Good as Its People*. He carried the right message at the right time—it was what people wanted to hear.

FROM PEANUTS TO THE PRESIDENCY

James Earl Carter Jr. was born in the small town of Plains, Georgia, on October 1, 1924, and grew up on his family's farm. Carter's mother, Lillian Gordy, was a strong presence at home and in her community, and she opposed the then-prevailing system of racial inequality. The future president was baptized in the conservative Southern Baptist Church. Carter often spoke of being a born-again Christian. (Born-again refers to having had a religious conversion experience in adulthood.) Despite his strong personal beliefs, he was committed to preserving the separation of church and state as implied by the First Amendment of the Constitution.

Carter graduated from the U.S. Naval Academy at Annapolis in 1946 and served in the navy's nuclear submarine program. In 1954, after his father's death, Carter resigned from the navy to take over the family's businesses, which included several thousand acres for growing peanuts. He remained active in the community and eventually entered politics.

THE ROAD TO THE WHITE HOUSE

Carter was elected to the Georgia State Senate in 1962 and became governor of Georgia in 1970. After deciding to run for president, he gained support from much of the old southern civil rights coalition and was endorsed by influential Representative Andrew Young, an African-American Democrat from Atlanta, Georgia, who had been the closest aide to the Reverend Martin Luther King Jr.

As a candidate, Carter enjoyed a broad appeal. He was popular with conservatives and liberals, African Americans and whites, the poor and the wealthy. After edging out a crowded field to take the Democratic nomination, Carter narrowly defeated President Ford and his running mate, Bob Dole, in the November 1976 election, taking 50.1 percent of the popular vote.

Bob Dole had a distinguished record of service in the Senate and as head of the Republican National Committee when he was Ford's running mate in 1976. *(Library of Congress)*

Jimmy Carter's mother, Lillian, was a great inspiration to him. (*Jimmy Carter Library*)

President Carter's interview with *Playboy* magazine caused controversy because the magazine was associated with Playboy clubs, where waitresses costumed as Playboy bunnies served drinks and food. Many people found the Playboy style demeaning to women. (*Sunbird Photos by Don Boyd*)

Carter's manner was down-to-earth and unpretentious. On Inauguration Day, he and his wife Rosalynn got out of their limousine and walked down Pennsylvania Avenue to the White House, and instead of wearing formal attire, he wore a blue suit. Carter was the first president to be sworn in using his nickname, Jimmy. During his first televised national address, Carter wore a cardigan sweater. No president had dressed so informally before on a national TV broadcast.

President Carter's family became well known during his term. He and Rosalynn had three sons, John William (known as Jack), James Earl III (Chip), and Donnel Jeffrey (Jeff). They also had a daughter, Amy, who was 9 years old when her father took office. The president's siblings, Gloria, Ruth, and Billy, and his mother, Lillian, became well-known figures too.

CARTER TAKES ACTION

Though his delivery was soft-spoken, Carter was a straight talker. In a press conference during his first year in office, Carter directly attacked oil companies for perpetrating "the biggest rip-off in history" in their manipulation of oil prices.

Some people believed that the straight-shooting Carter simply went too far with his honesty when, in an interview with *Playboy* magazine, he admitted that he had "lusted in [his] heart" after other women besides his wife. Carter was attempting to explain that he did not believe he should judge others, since he had had sinful impulses himself. In the article he also stated, "I have never been unfaithful to my wife." Carter received much criticism for discussing such a touchy subject with *Playboy*. (The magazine was known for sexually oriented content.) His honesty gained him both admirers and critics, and many felt that it hurt him politically by alienating potential supporters.

THE BICENTENNIAL

The United States celebrated the Bicentennial, or 200th anniversary, of the signing of the Declaration of Independence in an over-the-top manner that was uniquely American. Merchandisers had a field day, as commemorative trinkets of every imaginable sort were marketed to an eager public. Official stamps were issued, and special coins were minted with new designs for the backs of the 1976 quarter, half-dollar and silver dollar. The coins were dated 1776–1976. A number of plays, children's cartoons, and television specials focused on the American Revolution. A red, white, and blue theme could be seen everywhere from special patches on the uniforms of professional sports teams to repainted fire hydrants on city streets. A large regatta of historic ships, Operation Sail, traveled from port to port, gathering in New York City Harbor on July 4, 1976, for a review and celebration. Spectacular fireworks displays were held nationwide.

Americans enthusiastically celebrated the Bicentennial with parades, fireworks, and lots of merchandising. *(National Archives)*

When it came to implementing his ideas, Carter met with mixed success. His attempts to halt inflation and unemployment by raising interest rates met with opposition from Congress, and public dissatisfaction with the state of the economy and long gasoline lines led to frustration. Many assessments of Carter's term as president do point out positive elements, however. There was peace throughout his term, and no American died in combat.

Perhaps Carter's greatest personal achievement was in foreign policy. He helped create the Camp David Accords between Israel and Egypt, and the resulting treaty—the first between Israel and an Arab neighbor. The formal establishment of diplomatic relations and trade with China (building on President Nixon's efforts), and the agreement about transferring control of the Panama Canal to Panama were major achievements. Carter also worked for nuclear-arms control, and his concern for international human rights was credited with saving lives and reducing

The American Freedom Train toured the country in 1976, carrying the original versions of the U.S. Constitution, Declaration of Independence, and the Bill of Rights.

Carter signs an agreement on a visit to Mexico. He made foreign relations a priority early in his presidency. *(Jimmy Carter Library and Museum)*

torture. (He did receive criticism from some quarters for not doing enough for human rights.) Domestically, his environmental record was a major accomplishment. His judicial appointments won acclaim, and his 265 choices for the federal bench included many minority members and women.

Jimmy Carter appointed more African Americans to influential positions in the federal government than any president before him. However, the economic situation deteriorated under his presidency. The Congressional Black Caucus labeled Carter's federal budget, which favored military spending over domestic funding for social relief programs, "an unmitigated disaster" for African Americans. African-American unemployment had remained in double digits since the mid-1970s, twice the rate for whites.

"I want you to get up right now and go to the window. Open it, and stick your head out, and yell, 'I'm as mad as hell, and I'm not going to take this anymore!'"

—Actor Peter Finch, as news anchor Howard Beale, in the film *Network* (1976)

"INFLATION, DEFLATION, STAGNATION"

President Carter inherited a weak U.S. economy from his predecessor, President Ford. Taxes were high, inflation was out of control and prices kept rising, and business productivity was down. During periods of inflation, it seems to people that products suddenly become more expensive. What actually happens is that the value of money is deteriorating, which means it takes more money to buy the same product. When inflation rates are both high and erratic, as occurred during the Carter years, people tend to spend their salaries immediately rather than save them because the next month's inflation could be even higher. This lack of saving hinders banks' abilities to make loans and thereby hinders entrepreneurs' access to loans for their businesses, which reduces economic growth and can cause a recession, or period of reduced economic activity.

Immediately upon taking office, Carter declared that his primary domestic goal was to create jobs for the unemployed. The unemployment rate—or the number of unemployed workers divided by the total number of people able to work—had reached a high of 7.7 percent in 1976. At his request, Congress passed an Economic Stimulus Appropriations Act to create jobs

When the Organization of Petroleum Exporting Countries (OPEC), drastically cut back on sales to the United States, the limited supply forced Americans to face higher gas prices and long lines. Here, a young man waits to fill a gas can. *(Sarah Parvis)*

"If [a] civilization intercepts Voyager and can understand these recorded contents, here is our message: We are trying to survive our time so we may live into yours. We hope some day, having solved the problems we face, to join a community of Galactic Civilizations. This record represents our hope and our determination and our goodwill in a vast and awesome universe."

—President Jimmy Carter's statement placed on the *Voyager* spacecraft, June 16, 1977

MISSION TO MARS

NASA's unmanned *Viking* missions to Mars, in 1975, had three primary objectives: to obtain high-resolution pictures, to characterize the structure and composition of the atmosphere and surface, and to search for evidence of life. *Viking 1* was launched on August 1975 and arrived on Mars ten months later, in June 19, 1976. *Viking 2* was launched in September 1975 and entered Mars orbit in 1976.

The results from the Viking experiments gave scientists their most complete view of Mars to date. Volcanoes, lava plains, immense canyons, cratered areas, wind-formed features, and possible evidence of ancient surface water were apparent in the images. But alas . . . no Martians.

This photo of the Martian surface was sent back to Earth by one of the *Viking* missions. *(NASA)*

and help the economy. Unemployment declined, but the effects of huge price hikes in oil from the Middle East soon dominated the administration's domestic agenda. Due to the rise in oil prices, the cost of manufacturing almost everything from metal to plastics went up, and gas and fuel prices rose, too. Gas also became scarce, and many scientists predicted that the United States would run out of affordable energy to run its factories and cars within the next century or even the next few decades. These problems in all their complexity served to deepen the "Energy Crisis" that began during Nixon's second term. Carter found there was little the federal government could do to control inflation, which soon reached double-digit levels of more than 10 percent. A weak U.S. economy remained a stubborn issue in Carter's presidency.

AN ENERGY PLAN

The energy crisis continued to escalate during Carter's term as president. Making energy matters a top priority, he went before the American public a few months after his swearing in and told the American people that "75 percent of the oil and natural gas we rely on for energy is simply running out." Outlining a bold new plan to deal with the energy crisis, Carter told Congress that unless they accepted his plan, "We will face an economic, social and political crisis that will threaten our free institutions."

Equating the energy crisis with the "moral equivalent of war," the president pointed out to Americans that they were the greediest consumers of energy in the world. Energy conservation was a prominent element of his national energy plan. Carter pointed out that much U.S. energy consumption could be reduced by developing and using appliances and manufacturing equipment that used less energy to do the same tasks as more inefficient devices. He pointed out that conservation was the quickest, cheapest, most practical way of saving energy, and made it the cornerstone of his new policy.

The need for alternative energy sources became a political movement. Rallies to raise awareness of solar power were common during the 1970s.
(National Archives)

"The energy shortage was not inflicted on man by nature, but by his own illusions and mistakes."

—David Frum, author, *How We Got Here: The 1970s*

To encourage conservation, the president asked Congress to institute tax credits to reward responsible energy conservation with lower taxes. Tax credits were offered to individuals and businesses to motivate them to insulate their homes, stores, and factories, which would reduce energy used for heating and cooling. He lobbied Congress for a tax on gasoline to reduce gas consumption. He also proposed a tax on large, so-called gas guzzler cars.

MANAGING EXISTING ENERGY

Looking at the way Americans had consumed ever-increasing amounts of energy in the post–World War II years meant that the United States's energy needs would continue to grow. But the country could no longer produce all the energy it needed domestically. The United States simply did not have enough energy to supply itself. So the nation now was forced to import supplies from abroad, especially oil from the Middle East, which incurred high political, military, and economic costs.

Americans had become accustomed to the ability to secure inexpensive energy, and they neglected energy efficiency in favor of convenience and pleasure. Why ride the bus to work when driving a powerful car to work was more convenient, and when gasoline cost less than 30 cents per gallon? Why bother to spend money insulating one's house when oil and electricity prices hit record lows? As a result, energy demand grew, though supply did not.

Carter realized that if the growth in energy demand could be slowed, or even reduced, then the effects of the energy crisis could be mitigated. In short, he made energy conservation the most important element of his new policy and looked toward long-term energy independence rather than just a short-term fix to current woes.

A Palestinian wears a keffiyah, a symbol of Palestinian nationalism. The tense political situation in the Middle East made relying on oil from the area very risky for the United States. (*AP/Wide World*)

While conservation may have been the basis of his new policy, Carter also sought to develop other energy resources. He sought greater production of domestic coal and oil and explored the use of nuclear power plants, though he hoped the extra production could be achieved without adversely affecting the environment. Carter also hoped that alternative energy devices, such as solar cells, geothermal energy, and wind turbines, could become usable alternatives, and he pursued federal funding for their development.

A young couple prepare for their wedding ceremony in 1974. The sight was less common than it had been in the 1950s and 1960s, because many young people chose to live together rather than get legally married. *(National Archives)*

MARRIAGE V. POSSLQ

During the 1970s, the rate at which couples were getting married declined sharply. At the same time, divorce rates doubled from where they were in the 1950s, reaching an all-time high. As many young middle-class Americans watched their parents' marriages dissolve, they themselves stayed away from the institution of marriage. Some believed that it was a confining, repressive institution, especially for women. By 1980, almost 25 percent of American households contained only one person. Whatever position one took, either positive or negative, marriage as Americans understood it was eroding.

Many couples found an alternative to traditional marriage by living together. By 1979, more than 1 million households consisted of an unmarried man and woman. The U.S. Census Bureau designated such arrangements as POSSLQ (Persons of Opposite Sex Sharing Living Quarters). Though at one time this lifestyle would have been considered shocking, by the end of the decade much of the country agreed that it was morally acceptable for a man and woman to live together outside of marriage.

Mood rings were wildly popular. Many believed that blue or green indicated that the wearer had a warm and loving consciousness; however, the colors mainly indicated warm hands. *(Sarah Parvis)*

"It gave people a few moments of absolutely meaningless pleasure in a troubled world....If there were more fads there would probably be a lot fewer psychiatrists...."

—Ken Hakuta, author of *How to Create Your Own Fad and Make a Million Dollars,* discussing the Pet Rock

A DECADE OF FADS

Every decade seems to have its own fads—its own unique fashions, practices, or items that become extremely popular for a brief period, and then fade away just as abruptly. In addition to fads in music (disco) and fashion (leisure suits), the 1970s were filled with cultural artifacts like the Mood Ring and the Pet Rock.

Mood Rings appeared mid-decade as a must-have accessory and were popular with young people of both sexes. An invention of one Joshua Reynolds, Mood Rings contained a stone made of crystals that would change color depending on a number of factors, including the wearer's body temperature and temperature in the environment. The idea that the ring's hue expressed a person's current mood captured the imagination of a public looking to get in touch with their inner selves. The array of shifting colors was open to all manner of interpretation, a perfect fit in a decade when more and more people were seeking inner peace.

The Pet Rock was a marketing phenomenon that took absurd humor to new heights, peaking as a fad during the Christmas season in 1975. The brainstorm of a California advertising executive named Gary Dahl, the Pet Rock was was just that—a smooth round stone sold in a small cardboard box, complete with air holes, that resembled a pet carrier. The Pet Rock came with a clever book containing tongue-in-cheek instructions for caring for this unique pet, teaching them simple tricks ("sit" and "stay" being easy to master), and hints on naming and training them. The satirical sense of humor behind the Pet Rock shared a sensibility with the era's brand of self-referential comedy, such as that seen on television's *Saturday Night Live,* and seemed custom-made for the cynical 1970s.

CB RADIO

In the days before cellular phones, two-way Citizen's Band (or CB) Radio provided a way for individuals to communicate with each other while in vehicles. Used primarily by interstate truckers on the nation's highways, CB radios became a fad in the mid-1970s, helped along by the 1975 success of the popular song "Convoy" by C. W. McCall, and films such as *Smokey and the Bandit* (1977), which introduced Americans to the stylized lingo of CB users. Phrases such as "10-4, good buddy," (everything's okay), and words such as "Smokey" (police) found their way into common usage. (Smokeys received their nickname because their hats resembled the hat of Smokey the Bear, the mascot of the National Forest Service.)

There were initially 23 channels for CB users to chat on (increased to 40 in 1977), and enthusiasts used them at home as well as in their cars. Like the Internet chat rooms that became popular decades later, CB radio allowed people to get to know one another in a quasi-anonymous manner. All sorts of people adopted radio names, known as handles, among them Mrs. Betty Ford, who called herself First Mama.

SPORTS IN THE SPOTLIGHT

The 1970s were a time of expansion in the world of U.S. sports, as the major professional leagues of baseball, football, basketball, and ice hockey all added new franchises, and rival leagues sprouted up to challenge the status quo. The WFL (World Football League, 1974–75), WHA (World Hockey Association, 1972–79), and ABA (American Basketball Association, 1967–1976), all sought to attract fans in both new and established markets. The leagues all adopted rule changes to make their sports more appealing, and salaries for athletes soared, with the new leagues raiding the rosters of the established leagues and entering into bidding wars for top stars. Superstars such as football's Larry Csonka and hockey's Bobby Hull signed enormous contracts.

The ABA was perhaps the most successful of these renegade leagues when it came to capturing the public's imagination, despite operating on a shoestring budget. Its various franchises moved and went in and out of business on a consistent basis. At a time when basketball was not yet as popular as it would become in later decades, the ABA attracted fans with flashy gimmickry, cutting-edge coaching techniques, and creative, energetic individual play. Red, white, and blue basketballs, the invention of the three-point line,

Larry Csonka (left) of the Miami Dolphins, crashes over Minnesota Vikings cornerback Bobby Bryant in Super Bowl VIII in Houston, January 13, 1974. (*AP/Wide World*)

Julius Erving, wearing number 6, gets by Bill Walton on his way to scoring 24 points in the 1977 NBA championships. (*AP/Wide World*)

"Julius Erving was like Thomas Edison. He was inventing something new every night."

—Johnny Kerr, general manager of the Virginia Squires

scantily clad dancing girls, halftime cow-milking contests, and the high-flying exploits of players nicknamed Skywalker (David Thompson), Bad News (Marvin Barnes), and Eclipse (the impressively afro-haired Darnell Hillman). Julius Erving, known as Dr. J, became a popular figure, embodying the wild and wooly ABA style with a spectacular above-the-rim style of play that thrilled fans. Erving excelled with the Virginia Squires, and later led the New York Nets to two ABA Championships, winning the MVP award in 1974 and 1976.

The Howe family (left to right): Marty, Colleen, Mark, and Gordie, were the first family of hockey. Colleen worked in junior hockey; brothers Mark and Marty and father Gordie all had WHL contracts. (*AP/Wide World*)

The ABA eventually negotiated a merger with the NBA (National Basketball Association) for the 1976-77 season, which saw four teams—the Denver Nuggets, Indiana Pacers, New York (later New Jersey) Nets, and San Antonio Spurs—join the established league. Stars such as Erving, Moses Malone, and George "The Iceman" Gervin went on to excel in their new environs.

On the ice, the WHA merged with the NHL (National Hockey League) in 1979, and young stars such as Wayne Gretzky and Mark Messier and old legends such as Gordie Howe, (who had come out of retirement to join the new league in 1973), got to ply their trades before larger crowds. The WFL folded half way through the 1975 season, and the other leagues were on shaky financial ground before their mergers. Despite some degree of popularity, the new leagues were not a financial success.

At the 1976 Summer Olympics in Montreal, several American athletes became household names.

Bruce Jenner poses with his fiancé, Linda Thompson, an actress, on the popular syndicated TV series *Hee Haw.* Jenner went on to a lucrative career that included endorsements of products such as Wheaties as well as television appearances. (*AP/Wide World*)

Decathlon winner Bruce Jenner became a celebrity and went on to a television career, and three future world boxing champions emerged: "Sugar" Ray Leonard and the Spinks brothers, Michael and Leon. The undisputed star of these games, though, was fourteen-year-old Romanian gymnast Nadia Comaneci, who won three gold medals and not only became the first Olympic gymnast to be awarded a perfect score of 10, but repeated the feat six times.

CHAPTER 5

ADDRESSING HUMAN RIGHTS, 1977–1978

P RESIDENT CARTER STROVE TO MAKE human rights around the world a top priority in his adminstration's foreign policy. It was a challenging task. One of the ways that the Carter administration took a stand for human rights was to end support to the U.S.-backed dictatorship of the Somoza family in the Central American country of Nicaragua.

President Carter speaks with the shah of Iran, Reza Pahlevi, in the White House in 1977.
(Jimmy Carter Presidential Library)

By 1977, the first oil pumped through the Trans-Alaska Pipeline System reached Valdez, Alaska.

The Trans-Alaska Pipeline System began operating in 1977, after years of opposition from environmentalists who feared its construction and use would damage the fragile Arctic landscape. *(U.S. Army Corps of Engineers)*

President Jimmy Carter signed legislation creating the U.S. Department of Energy in 1977.

The Somoza family had ruled Nicaragua for decades, exploiting the nation's people and its resources for their own gain. The first member of the Somoza family had gained the presidency in 1936, supported by U.S. Marines, who had been sent to the country to protect American business interests and preserve order. A number of Somozas held power throughout the following decades. But after Carter cut U.S. support to the Somoza regime, the country experienced a civil war. The Sandinistas were the main revolutionary group opposed to the U.S.-backed regime.

A major conflict between human rights and U.S. strategic interests came in Carter's dealings with the shah of Iran, Reza Pahlevi. The shah was the hereditary ruler of Iran, one of the world's last monarchies. Iran is a large, oil-rich nation in the Middle East. (In ancient times, it was known as Persia.) Iran had been a strong ally of the United States since World War II, and was one of the few U.S.-friendly regimes in the area. However, the shah had unlimited power. There were no free elections in Iran, nor freedom of the press. Outwardly, Carter praised the shah as a wise leader. Yet, when a popular uprising against the monarchy broke out in Iran, the Carter administration did not intervene.

The shah was removed from office, exiled from his county, and never allowed to return. Many have considered the shah's dwindling support from the United States a major cause of his rapid overthrow.

The new government was ruled by the Ayatollah Khomeini, a high-ranking Shiite Muslim religious authority who established a new constitution giving himself supreme powers. (Ayatollah is a religious title, like reverend or archbishop.) Carter was initially prepared to recognize the revolutionary government of the monarch's successor, but his efforts proved futile. The new government was rabidly anti-American. "Americans are the great Satan, the wounded snake," said the ayatollah.

BILLY CARTER

While President Carter's sister Ruth Carter Stapleton gained recognition as a Christian evangelist, his younger brother, Billy Carter, achieved his own kind of fame during his sibling's tenure in the White House. A colorful and outspoken character, Billy Carter was considered unpredictable and less eloquent and refined than his brother, a reputation that was not helped much by his actions. Billy wrote a book called *Redneck Power*, produced his own brand of beer (Billy Beer, with which he was pictured on the November 14, 1977, cover of *Newsweek*), and was often portrayed as a country bumpkin by the media.

In a controversial development, Billy visited the oil-rich North African country of Libya with a group of investors several times in

Billy Carter, the president's brother, was investigated for influence peddling, but he was not indicted on or convicted of any illegal activity. (*Jimmy Carter Library and Museum*)

1978. Relations between Libya and the United States were strained at the time. The Libyan government had been accused of state-sponsored terrorism, and the United States had imposed trade sanctions earlier that year. In addition to creating a major embarrassment for his brother the president, the incident led to a Senate investigation (dubbed Billygate) that looked into allegations of influence peddling. (Influence peddling is the practice of using one's influence with persons in power to obtain favors or preferential treatment usually in return for payment.) It was revealed that Billy had received hundreds of thousands of dollars in consultant fees from the Libyan government.

THE CAMP DAVID SUMMIT

When Jimmy Carter entered the White House in 1977, there had been four wars between the Arab states and Israel since the founding of the Jewish state in 1948. The Six Day War of 1967 had ended with an Israeli victory, and Israel gained possession of land that had once belonged to Egypt, (the Gaza Strip and Sinai Peninsula), Syria (the Golan Heights) and Jordan (East Jerusalem, and Judea and Samaria—also known as the West Bank). The surprise attack on Israel that precipitated the Yom Kippur War of 1973 had not brought about any comprehensive peace settlement and had not helped Israel's Arab neighbors regain any of the land that had been lost in the earlier war.

President Carter recognized that continuing problems in the Middle East could increase the tension between the United States and the Soviet Union, because both nations wanted to maintain their access to the oil

"You are not a realist unless you believe in miracles."

—Egyptian president Anwar-el Sadat, 1977

resources there. The Soviets were backing the Arab nations with money and weapons. President Carter was deeply committed to supporting Israel. "The Judeo-Christian ethic and study of the Bible were bonds between Jews and Christians which had always been part of my life," he stated. "I also believed very deeply that the Jews who had survived the Holocaust deserved their own nation, and that they had a right to live in peace among their neighbors."

INITIATING PEACE TALKS

Carter's efforts toward bringing peace to the Middle East began during a period of better relations between Arabs and Israelis. In November 1977, the president of Egypt, Anwar Sadat, made history as the first Arab leader to visit Israel. President Sadat undertook the visit under near-universal condemnation by other Arab leaders, who refused to negotiate with or even recognize Israel. He was called a traitor to the Arab cause, but Sadat saw his visit to Israel as a way to begin a dialogue that could result in a peace treaty and return the Sinai Peninsula to Egyptian sovereignty.

After years as a Soviet ally, the Egyptian economy was ailing, and regaining the Sinai would not only be a boost to Egypt's morale but also a catalyst in obtaining financial aid from the United States. For Israel, the prospect of a peace treaty with a formerly hostile neighbor was an important element of national security.

Sadat was welcomed by his former adversaries, and Israeli president Menachem Begin reciprocated with a visit to Egypt during the following year. However, despite apparent willingness of many Arabs and Israelis, the leaders on both sides were having trouble talking and finding ways to compromise.

Left to right: Aliza Begin, President Carter, Prime Minister Begin, and First Lady Rosalynn Carter stand at a toast during a state visit. *(National Archives)*

In August 1978, President Carter sent Secretary of State Cyrus Vance to the Middle East to invite the leaders to Camp David, the presidential retreat located in Maryland. Camp David has often been used for formal and informal discussion between United States and world leaders. When Carter's advisers suggested that he try only to outline a plan for peace with Sadat and Begin at Camp David, Carter replied, "You are not aiming high enough." He said that at the very least, there needed to be a peace treaty between Egypt and Israel. He added that "by getting them to Camp David, away from the press and out of the glare of publicity and away from their own political constituencies, I think I can bring them to understand each other's positions better."

Secretary of State Cyrus Vance (left) was instrumental in helping President Carter set up the historic Camp David summit. *(National Archives)*

TROUBLE AT THE TALKS

The Camp David summit, as it came to be known, took place between September 5 and 17, 1978, and was not always peaceful itself. Only a few days in, Carter's strategy had unraveled. Sadat started the negotiations with a hard-line agenda; Begin hardly seemed interested in making a deal at all. There were times when Carter's role seemed like that of a referee. "It was mean," he told his wife, Rosalynn. "They were brutal with each other, personal."

Despite the difficulties, Carter was determined not to give up. He decided that if Sadat and Begin could not talk to each other, they would have to communicate through him. From then on, the United States would not only be the mediator but would also be an active participant in the negotiations.

Begin hands Carter a humorous note, combining the Hebrew word for peace, *shalom*, with Carter's Southern drawl. Carter's personal relationship with the Middle Eastern leaders proved crucial in the peace process. *(National Archives)*

It was Carter's determination that kept the talks going, even when it looked like there was no hope. For example, after eleven days of negotiations Egyptian president Sadat told U.S. secretary of state Vance that he was leaving. Upon hearing this, Carter told Sadat: "Our friendship is over. You promised me that you would stay at Camp David as long as I was willing to negotiate...I consider this a serious blow...to the relationship between Egypt and the United States."

Sadat agreed to stay. Next, Israeli president Begin threatened to withdraw from the agreement over the wording of a letter. Carter managed to soothe Begin by autographing photos for Begin's grandchildren. The Israeli was moved by this gesture and agreed to accept a new draft of the disputed letter.

CARTER'S ROLE

The president acted as lead negotiator, going back and forth between Sadat and Begin. Sadat, who would develop a strong friendship with Carter, favored a bold approach, and gave Carter a lot of creative control in crafting a deal that the Israelis might accept. Begin, on the other hand, argued over every word, and seemed

President Carter shakes hands with Egyptian president Anwar Sadat and Israeli prime minister Menachem Begin. *(Library of Congress)*

less willing to compromise. So Carter tactfully went around Begin to more flexible members of the Israeli negotiating team. With the Egyptians he did the opposite, going straight to Sadat.

Another key tactic was Carter's decision to separate out some of the key issues and produce two documents laying out the plan for peace, instead of one. The first was a peace treaty between Egypt and Israel, in which both countries compromised on certain issues. Israel agreed to withdraw from the Sinai and return the area to Egyptian control, while Egypt agreed to restrictions on the number of troops it could place there, and guaranteed Israeli vessels safe passage through important shipping lanes in the Suez Canal and Straits of Tirian. The second document laid out principles for future negotiations that would address issues such as Palestinian autonomy and the future of the Gaza Strip.

A shining moment of Jimmy Carter's presidency occurred on Monday, September 18, 1978. With Sadat and Begin watching from a balcony, Carter briefed a joint session of Congress on their thirteen-day summit at Camp David. He received twenty-five minutes of applause. "Blessed are the peacemakers, for they shall be the children of God," reflected an emotional Carter.

The six-month period following the signing proved just how fragile the agreement really was. Many smaller details that still needed to be worked out proved to be big stumbling blocks. In March, Carter flew to the Middle East in an effort to save the accords. On March 26, 1979, the White House hosted a signing ceremony for the Israel-Egypt Peace Treaty before 1,600 assembled guests.

The Camp David agreement was Carter's most important presidential accomplishment and established him as a global statesman. Carter's ethics of hard work, attention to detail, moral integrity, and determination were all important contributions to the success of the summit. "There will never be a history of the

"Camp David is the beginning of a process that still goes on. And a hundred years from now, two hundred years from now, people will be talking about the . . . process that began in those Maryland mountains."

—Historian Douglas Brinkley, on the 1978 Camp David accords

On March 27, 1977, a pair of 747 airliners collided on a runway in Tenerife, in the Canary Islands, killing 560 people. It is the worst air disaster of the 20th century and the single most deadly accident in aviation history.

Middle East written without Jimmy Carter's name in the index," says historian Douglas Brinkley.

Americans felt proud of the peace-making role their nation had played on the world stage. At the time, events in the Middle East loomed large in the minds of U.S. residents; the energy crisis showed how much of U.S. daily life relied upon steady supplies of oil and stability in a region far from America's shores. But events closer to home soon captured center stage.

PANAMA CANAL TREATY

Since 1903, the United States had controlled a narrow strip of land in the small Central American nation of Panama, where the Panama Canal passed through. Some Central Americans felt that the U.S. control of the land was unwelcome and invasive—a remnant of colonialism.

The United States had originally gained control of the land by supporting Panamanian revolutionaries in their quest for independence from Colombia. In 1904, the U.S. began digging a 51-mile shortcut between the Atlantic and Pacific oceans through the new country and called it the Panama Canal. Before the canal opened in 1914, ships traveling between the Atlantic and Pacific had had to travel 8,000 nautical miles around the tip of South America. The canal was tremendously important to the development of the western United States and to world trade. However, the U.S.-controlled land in the middle of an otherwise independent nation irritated many Central and South Americans.

By the 1970s, Panamanian calls for sovereignty over the Canal Zone had reached high pitch, and U.S. relations with Panama deteriorated. President Carter saw returning the Panama Canal to the government of Panama as key to improving U.S. relations in the southern hemisphere and the developing world. On September 7, 1977, President Jimmy Carter signed the

A U.S. Coast Guard ship passes through the Panama Canal. Some U.S. military and political advisers opposed turning the strategically important canal over to Panamanian authority, but Carter set the process in motion with the Panama Canal Treaty of 1977. *(NOAA)*

Panama Canal Treaty and Neutrality Treaty promising to give control of the canal to the Panamanians by the year 2000.

The Panama Canal Treaties of 1977–1978 meant to rectify a long-term issue of argument between the United States and Latin America. Opponents of returning the canal to Panama by 2000 criticized Carter's efforts. They felt that since the United States had paid for building the canal, it should maintain control. The treaties narrowly passed the Senate in April 1978. Although U.S. relations with Panama were cordial into the early 1980s, by the mid-1980s, relations with Panama deteriorated under the leadership of General Manuel Antonio Noriega.

THE PRESIDENT'S WORKING PARTNER

As first lady, Rosalynn Carter participated in political affairs to an extent that was unmatched by any of the president's wives before her. With the exception of President Franklin Roosevelt's wife, Eleanor, the first lady had remained seen and not heard, especially on policy issues. However, Rosalynn attended cabinet meetings when the subject under discussion interested her, and she and the president scheduled daily working lunches.

First Lady Rosalynn Carter was a very active partner in her husband's administration. Some questioned her role in trade and diplomatic visits to Caribbean and Latin American countries. *(Library of Congress)*

A group of young adults rest on a lawn, awaiting a free pop concert in Maryland. Many observers thought that the young people of the 1970s were less politically and socially engaged than those of the 1960s, and their music reflected this. *(Sarah Parvis)*

"We are now in the Me Decade—seeing the upward roll of the third great religious wave in American history."

—Author Tom Wolfe, 1976

In June 1977, Rosalynn Carter visited several countries in the Caribbean and Latin America, meeting with their leaders to discuss important matters relating to trade and defense. Even though there were reports that she performed well, some questioned whether she should have taken on such a high-profile role, because she had not been elected or appointed to any official position representing the United States. Mrs. Carter also traveled abroad for ceremonial occasions and on humanitarian missions, such as a trip to a refugee camp in Cambodia in 1979.

THE ME DECADE

Though the economic situation in the United States seemed grim at times during the 1970s, the great majority of Americans remained dedicated to leisure activities and self-expression. With polarizing and painful realities such as the war in Vietnam, and the Watergate scandal receding into memory, a sensibility emerged that found many Americans concentrating on a path of fulfilling their own personal happiness. A great number of people seemed to focus less on political and social issues and more on personal well-being and the pursuit of individuality. This led some to term the 1970s the Me decade.

State of the art gadgetry such as cable television and digital watches were quickly adopted in some social circles. In California, luxurious hot tubs for relaxing and socializing became both a staple and a status symbol for those who could afford them. The dream of personal improvement was a much sought after goal, and a desire for new ways of achieving enlightenment led people to experiment with different types of psychological work. Many joined encounter groups, group therapy sessions, or even cults as a way of finding themselves or at least helping them achieve a sense of balance in an increasingly fragmented society.

> **A major power blackout in New York City on July 13, 1977 lasted for 25 hours and resulted in looting, arson, and widespread disorder.**

THE 1950s RETURN

Like the decade preceding them, the 1970s were a time with no shortage of turmoil. Perhaps it was a longing for what may have seemed a simpler, less stressful time, or maybe it was a longing for the fashion, the music, or the social mores of a decade that seemed far away. Whatever the cause, the 1970s saw a big boom in 1950s-era nostalgia.

Happy Days, a television comedy set in Milwaukee, Wisconsin, in the latter part of the 1950s, first aired on ABC in 1974. It featured a typical family of four: mother, father, older brother Ritchie and younger sister Joanie (another brother, Chuck, mysteriously disappeared after the first season). Many of the scenes took place in an archetypical drive-in diner. By 1976, it was the most popular show on television and spawned a number of spin-offs, one of which, *Laverne and Shirley,* followed it to the top of the Nielsen ratings.

The musical group Sha Na Na achieved fame reworking doo-wop standards from the 1950s and were rewarded with their own television variety show, while *Grease,* a musical about 1950s teenagers, played to sellout crowds on Broadway from 1972 through the end of the decade. *Grease* was made into a 1978 movie starring John Travolta and Olivia Newton-John that was a tremendous box office success.

The popularity of such TV shows as *Happy Days* reflected a fascination with the pop culture of what appeared to have been a simpler time. *(National Archives)*

TOGA PARTIES

In 1978, *Newsweek* magazine reported that hundreds of college campuses were holding Roman-style toga parties. In fact, at the University of Wisconsin there was a single toga party with 10,000 attendees. What would cause tens of thousands of young people to wrap themselves in bed sheets and don a wreath on their heads in the style of the ancient Greeks and Romans? Why, a movie, of course! National Lampoon's *Animal House* was released in 1978. It starred John Belushi, a featured cast member in the immensely popular television show *Saturday Night Live.* In the movie, Belushi and his buddies engage in raucous behavior, including fraternity hazing and campus food fights. In one scene, they dressed themselves in bed sheets and laurel wreaths—and the toga party craze was born.

Elvis Presley died on August 16, 1977, at Graceland, his home in Memphis, Tennessee.

A line of cars follows the hearse bearing Elvis Presley's body to the Forest Hills Cemetery in Memphis, Tennessee. *(AP/Wide World)*

POPULAR PERSONALITIES

A number of larger-than-life figures flourished in the popular imagination of U.S. citizens during the Me decade. Celebrities became ever more visible as nationwide broadcast and cable television brought ever-larger audiences together. Motorcycle daredevil Evel Knievel captured the imagination of a generation of American youngsters by making spectacular televised leaps over rows of buses, tanks of sharks, and unsuccessfully, Idaho's Snake River Canyon aboard a specially designed rocket-cycle in September 1974.

In the world of spectator sports, professional football reached unparalleled popularity, as successful teams such as the Dallas Cowboys and Pittsburgh Steelers established coast-to-coast followings. Football began to rival baseball as the country's national pastime in the eyes of fans. Major League Baseball underwent a number of changes with far-reaching consequences. The American League adapted the designated hitter rule in 1973, which aroused controversy as it changed the strategy of the game by allowing an extra non-fielding batter to replace the pitcher in the line-up when a team came up to bat. The National League did not adopt the rule; its pitchers still came to the plate when it was their turn to bat.

An even bigger change occurred on December 23, 1975, when a legal arbitrator overruled baseball's reserve clause, which bound a player to his team, establishing the notion of free agency. Previously, a baseball player could not choose to sign with any team. Once a team signed a player, he was theirs for life, unless they traded him. Free agency meant that a player whose contract with a team ran out was free to sign with another team.

Great bidding wars broke out for stars that became free agents. The New York Yankees set the pace in signing a number of productive free agents and went on to win three pennants in the latter half of the decade, as well as the 1977 and 1978 World Series. Among the charismatic players who signed as free agents with the Yankees were popular pitcher Jim "Catfish" Hunter, and slugger Reggie Jackson, whose outspoken charm and success at the plate led to a brand of candy, the Reggie! Bar, being named after him.

"If I was playing in New York, they'd name a candy bar after me."

—Oakland A's outfielder
Reggie Jackson predicts
the future, 1973

Slugger Reggie Jackson, one of the more outspoken and prominent baseball personalities of the late 1970s, celebrates the Yankees 1977 World Series win at the introduction of the Reggie! Bar, named after him. *(AP/Wide World)*

"May the Force Be with You."

—Obi-Wan Kenobi (Alec Guinness) utters the motto of the Jedi Knights, in the 1977 movie *Star Wars*

BIRTH OF THE BLOCKBUSTER

By mid-decade, a major development in the realm of popular film was the "blockbuster movie," an expensively made film marked by its large production costs and spectacular, sophisticated special effects. These heavily promoted, big-budget extravaganzas, spearheaded by Steven Spielberg's *Jaws* (1976) and George Lucas's *Star Wars* (1977), opened to huge crowds and attendant hoopla, and inspired numerous tie-ins, such as games, T-shirts, and posters. Later in the decade, movies such as Michael Cimino's *The Deer Hunter* (1978) and Coppola's *Apocalypse Now* (1979) addressed the horrors of the Vietnam War for the first time.

The 1977 release of *Star Wars* touched off a pop-culture phenomenon. Filmgoers became fascinated with the thrill-filled futuristic saga, which harkened back to the science-fiction serials of the 1930s and 1940s. The story of young Luke Skywalker's quest struck a chord in viewers, who lined up to see the movie over and over again. Original characters such as R2D2, Darth Vader, and Chewbacca became household names, and the film spawned sequels, books, comics, and video games. By 2005, *Forbes* magazine estimated the overall revenue generated by the entire *Star Wars* franchise was nearly $20 billion, making it the most successful film franchise ever.

Left to right: Harrison Ford, Anthony Daniels, Carrie Fisher, and Peter Mayhew appeared in the phenomenally popular movie *Star Wars*. Ford and Fisher went on to stardom; Anthony Daniels, who played the robot C-3PO, and Mayhew, who played Chewbacca, an alien Wookie, were so heavily costumed that they did not become as instantly recognizable as their costars. *(AP/Wide World)*

CHAPTER 6

OPTIMISM, ESCAPISM, AND DISILLUSIONMENT, 1978–1979

THE LATE 1970s WERE A TIME OF optimism in international affairs. U.S. soldiers were not at war, and the possibility of peace in the Middle East seemed achievable. At home, however, the American economy continued to weaken, inflation continued, and oil prices kept rising. A number of national issues dominated the news, and Americans found pleasure and escapism in new forms of music and entertainment.

A racially diverse group of college students gather informally in 1978. By the late 1970s, African-American enrollment in U.S. colleges and universities had risen. The *Regents of the University of California v. Bakke* case highlighted some of the racial tensions made evident by this change in demographics. *(Sarah Parvis)*

"The cumulative effect... is that no one has a legal right to have any demographic characteristic they possess be considered a favorable point on their behalf, but an employer has a right to take into account the goals of the organization and the interests of American society in making decisions."

—Representative Mark B. Cohen of Philadelphia, on *Regents of the University of California v. Bakke,* 1978

"We must adjust to changing times and still hold to unchanging principles."

—U.S. president Jimmy Carter addresses the nation, 1977

REGENTS OF THE UNIVERSITY OF CALIFORNIA v. BAKKE

During the 1970s, the Supreme Court decided several landmark cases that helped support the efforts of the U.S. Equal Employment Opportunity Commission (EEOC). The EEOC's goal is to eliminate illegal discrimination from the workplace for all workers. The Supreme Court, as the most powerful court in the United States, is the last stop for cases appealed from lower courts. One of the most controversial Supreme Court case decided during the 1970s was known as *Regents of the University of California v. Bakke.*

Allan Bakke, a 35-year-old white student, was rejected twice from the University of California Medical School. He believed the University of California was in violation of the Fourteenth Amendment's equal protection clause and the 1965 Civil Rights Act because his grade point average and test scores were higher than those of any minority student accepted during the two years he applied. As part of a program called affirmative action, the school reserved 16 out of 100 openings for minority students, and therefore, Bakke argued, his rejections were based solely on his race.

The justices were mixed in their response, but on June 28, 1978, they ruled that race could be an allowable factor considered in choosing a diverse student body in university admissions decisions. The court also held, however, that the use of quotas (or reserving openings for minority students) was not permissible. Therefore, by maintaining a 16 percent minority quota, the University of California had discriminated against Bakke. As a result of the decision, Bakke was admitted to the medical school and graduated in 1992.

"Race or ethnic background may be deemed a 'plus' in a particular applicant's file, yet it does not insulate the individual from comparison with all other candidates for the available seats," said Supreme Court Justice Lewis F. Powell, explaining the decisions.

THE EQUAL RIGHTS AMENDMENT (ERA)

The Equal Rights Amendment (ERA) was a proposed amendment to the Constitution. It would have guaranteed equal rights under law for all Americans regardless of gender. It read in part: "Equality of rights under the law shall not be denied or abridged by the United States or by any state on account of sex." Debate about the necessity, indeed even the constitutionality, of the ERA came to a head in 1979.

Although the amendment had been proposed in 1923, three years after the ratification of the Nineteenth Amendment, which gave women the right to vote, it was not approved by Congress and given to the states for ratification until 1972. (Ratification means that each state votes to accept the amendment as part of the Constitution.) Congress had set a seven-year time limit for ratification, and 38 states needed to ratify the ERA. But by the end of that deadline in 1979 only 35 of the 38 required states had done so. In

Following the 1978 murder of Mayor George Moscone and openly gay city supervisor Harvey Milk, Dianne Feinstein becomes the first woman mayor of San Francisco, California.

A group of women supporting equal rights march from Farragut Square to Lafayette Park in Washington, D.C., during one of the demonstrations for equal rights in the 1970s. Feminists were sometimes disparagingly referred to as women's libbers, because they supported women's liberation from strict societal roles. *(Library of Congress)*

Outside the White House, women opposed to the Equal Rights Amendment hold signs. Although most women did not want to be oppressed by unequal laws, some did not think an amendment to the constitution was required to achieve equality under the law. *(Library of Congress)*

"What I am defending is the real rights of women. A woman should have the right to be in the home as a wife and mother."

—ERA opponent
Phyllis Schlafly, 1978

fact, 5 of those approving states actually later rescinded, or took back, their ratifications. In 1978, as the 1979 deadline loomed near, Congress extended the ratification deadline until 1982, but no further states ratified the proposed amendment during that additional period.

The political climate changed in the late 1970s, and the Republican Party withdrew its earlier bipartisan support for the ERA. Political opposition to the ERA was led by Phyllis Schlafly, a conservative author and activist. The ERA would have granted more power to Congress and the federal courts at a time when public opposition to judicial activism, or involvement in lawmaking, was growing.

Schlafly went on to become the most visible and effective opponent of the ERA; she organized the Stop ERA movement. Schlafly argued that the amendment would actually take away important family rights for women, such as automatic child custody in the case of divorce, and would also make young women subject to the military draft. She also maintained that if passed, the amendment would lead to unisex bathrooms, taxpayer-funded abortions, and same-sex marriage. Her actions were widely criticized by younger feminists, who denounced her as a subservient housewife who personified everything the feminist movement was seeking to overcome.

THE BIRTH OF BIOTECHNOLOGY

It was in 1953 that scientists James Watson and Francis Crick conceived the double helix model of DNA (deoxyribonucleic acid), thus unlocking the means for understanding this basic molecular blueprint of life. (DNA controls how living things reproduce, develop, and operate.) Their discovery opened the door to the devel-

American Isaac Bashevis Singer won the 1978 Nobel Prize for Literature.

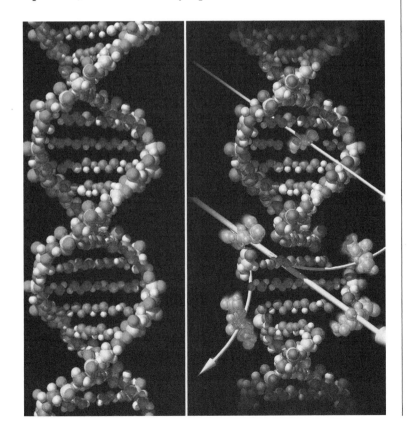

A sophisticated computer model shows the double helix structure of DNA, as well as how it can be damaged. Biotechnology research took a big step forward when scientists discovered how to cut apart and reassemble parts of the DNA molecule. *(NASA)*

"There were real gas lines, there was real inflation... people were worried in their real lives about keeping their jobs. We could engage the nation by addressing those problems and asking for a new level of public support."

—Vice President
Walter Mondale, 1978

opment of biotechnology, or the manipulation of biological processes by humans for their own purposes. However, it was not until the 1970s that scientists began to see how biotechnology research and applications might really help in the treatment of human disease. The United Nations defines *biotechnology* as "any technological application that uses biological systems, living organisms, or derivatives thereof, to make or modify products or processes for specific use."

In the early 1970s, the federal government charged researchers with the task of advancing the

THE FIRST COMPUTER BULLETIN BOARD

In 1978, the first computer bulletin board system (BBS) was created. A BBS runs software that allows users to dial into the system over a phone line to download software and data, upload data, read news, and exchange messages with other users. During their heyday, which began in the late 1970s, many BBSes were run as a hobby. The people who ran them were called sysops, or system operators, while other BBSes charged their users money. Before the Internet was home to chat rooms, online services, and newsgroups, BBS served as online forums to connect people around the country and around the world.

The Apple II+ model personal computer, introduced in June 1979, was one of the earliest personal computers on the market. It appealed mainly to hobbyists at the time. *(Computer Closet)*

FIRST TEST-TUBE BABY

On July 25, 1978, Louise Joy Brown, the world's first successful so-called test-tube baby, was born in Manchester, England. Though the technology that made her conception possible was a triumph in medicine and science and since then has become commonly used, at the time some people considered the procedure controversial.

The process involved the fertilization of the mother's egg by the father's sperm outside the body, in a laboratory (thus the terms *test tube,* or *in vitro,* Latin for "in glass"). The resulting embryo was then implanted in the mother's womb.

Weighing 5 pounds, 12 ounces, baby Louise was delivered by caesarean section. The first successful in-vitro fertilization (IVF) treatment in in the United States took place three years later, and there have been tens of thousands of babies born with the aid of IVF treatment since then.

---

frontiers of genetic research to aid in the war on cancer. This served to sow the seed of a new industry. By the late 1970s, scientists in California had developed techniques that enabled scientists to cut genetic material from the cells of one organism, and then paste it into another organism. This was an important discovery because the genetic material they moved from one place to another instructs a cell as to how to make a particular protein. The organism that receives the cells is then able to make that protein. Over time, scientists have perfected the technique of splicing material that enables cells to create proteins that control the creation of insulin, the level of blood pressure, and many other human functions.

The 1978 Nobel Prize for medicine went to Dr. Hamilton O. Smith and Dr. Daniel Nathans of Johns Hopkins University of the United States, and Professor Werner Arber of Switzerland. The prize was awarded for discovering enzymes that act like biological scissors. The enzymes cut DNA into pieces, an essential tool in genetic research.

DISCO RISING

Disco music, with origins in funk and soul, emerged during the 1970s as a full blown cultural movement. Disco became the most prominent form of popular

Mirrored disco balls became a familiar prop in clubs throughout the country, as well as many high school dances and proms. (*Sarah Parvis*)

music at the time and flourished largely only during the decade. This differentiates it from pop, rock, classical, jazz, folk, and other forms of music.

A form of dance music that emerged from the gay and African-American subcultures, disco featured syncopated rhythms at a faster tempo—more beats per minute—than previous dance-oriented genres. Popular recordings were played in dance clubs (discotheques) and often remixed on twelve-inch records that were spun on turntables as people performed a variety of popular dance steps such as the hustle on the disco floor. The discos themselves featured all manner of inventive lighting and design, including strobe lights, suspended giant mirrored balls, and smoke machines. Fashion, too, played a part in the disco experience with distinctive styles such as wide lapel suits, gold lamé tops, and platform shoes spreading into the mainstream as disco's popularity steadily rose from 1975 to the end of the decade.

One of the most successful disco groups was the Bee Gees, who hailed from Australia and revived a

Three brothers, Robin, Maurice, and Barry Gibb, formed the Bee Gees, one of the most successful groups of all time. Their danceable disco hits dominated the charts in the late 1970s. *(Sunbird Photos by Don Boyd)*

DISCO DEMOLITION NIGHT

In the late 1970s, disco bashing became a major preoccupation among certain segments of the population. "Disco Sucks" was the motto of choice for many music fans who preferred the harder guitar sounds of rock music. On July 12, 1979, a Chicago radio station organized a promotional event, dubbed "Disco Demolition Night," in Comiskey Park during a Chicago White Sox double header. People were admitted for reduced admission and encouraged to bring disco records to the ballpark, where the offending vinyl would be destroyed in the outfield with explosives between games. Things degenerated after the records were blown up, as thousands of inebriated fans stormed the field and wandered the stands setting fires and the evening devolved into chaos. The White Sox had to forfeit the second game when order could not be sufficiently restored.

previously successful pop music career with a number of top hits in the disco mold. Three of their biggest hits were featured on the soundtrack to the movie *Saturday Night Fever,* which became the top selling album in history to that point. The film, starring actor John Travolta as a rebellious young Italian-American from Brooklyn, New York, featured a gritty, realistic plot and dynamic dance scenes set in a local disco. It became the biggest impetus for the disco craze among the mainstream public.

Singer Donna Summer was known as the Queen of Disco, establishing herself as a star with a succession of number one records. Another group that came to be identified with disco was the Village People. Performing songs such as "YMCA" in their trademark costumes, the group was very popular in the gay community but made a successful transition to become favorites in mainstream America.

While it is often looked down upon by much of the public today, disco was a very powerful fad in the seventies, and its effects persisted, influencing the hip-hop and electronic dance music that developed in the 21st century.

Sony introduces the Walkman, the first portable stereo, in 1978. Originally rather large (one listener recalls his non-Sony version as "about the size of a Girl Scout cookie box") and expensive, new versions became smaller and cheaper, spurring music sales across all genres.

PUNK

Another musical development that reached the United States by the end of the 1970s was punk rock. Angry, provocative, loud and fast, punk rock was very much a reaction to the complacent and somewhat bloated state of the music industry, and much of society and the establishment in general. At a time when millionaire rock stars flew around the world in Lear-jets and composed ever more self-indulgent and excessively orchestrated works, punk rock was a stripped down alternative.

Although the term *punk* was first coined by magazine editors in the United States, and the beginnings of the punk movement may have stirred in America back in the 1960s, it was in England that punk first became a full-fledged subculture. With spiked hair or

PUNK TRAILBLAZERS

The Sex Pistols were the most notorious of the punk bands, going out of their way to embody the ethos of rebellion and project an attitude of nihilistic excess— an attitude that society and life itself are senseless and useless. Lead singer John Lydon, aka "Johnny Rotten," seemed to delight in behaving badly for the media, but also challenged the prevailing belief system and opened up topics from politics to religion to debate. The drug use and rock 'n' roll lifestyle caught up with the band, however. They released just one album, *Never Mind the Bollocks* (1977), and disbanded in 1978 after an undisciplined U.S. tour. On October 12, 1978, the group's bassist Sid Vicious, who embodied a punk rock archetype with a reputation for drug abuse, violence, and other unpleasant behavior, was arrested for allegedly stabbing his girlfriend Nancy Spungen to death in their room at Manhattan's Chelsea Hotel. Vicious was out on bail for this, and a subsequent assault rap, when he overdosed on heroin and died on February 2, 1979. Despite the brevity of their existence, the Sex Pistols influenced many American bands.

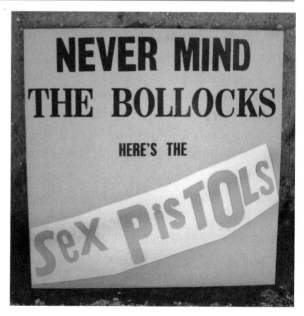

The Sex Pistol's first and only album, *Never Mind the Bollocks,* became an instant classic, featuring such songs as "God Save the Queen." *(Flora Carnevale)*

mohawks, ripped clothing, boots, and body parts pierced by safety pins, adherents of the punk aesthetic adopted a confrontational appearance. Initially the movement was political as much as it was a fashion statement, and the message seemed to be a rejection of current social values. It can be argued that the craze was at least in part kicked off by a tour of the country by the legendary New York band The Ramones, in 1976. The Ramones' tour influenced an entire crop of young British music makers who went on to form bands including The Clash, The Damned, and the Sex Pistols. Both abroad and in the United States, the punk movement very much involved a do-it-yourself attitude, centered on the belief that everything from playing music to promoting shows and releasing recordings could be done by anyone who wanted to do so, rather than going through the processes of the corporate music world.

In the United States, punk evolved on both coasts and in many places, both small and large, in between. The epicenter for this nascent music, though, was New York City, where the narrow bar CBGB (for Country,

"Don't accept the old order. Get rid of it."

—Singer Johnny Rotten of the Sex Pistols, 1978

CBGBs on the Bowery in New York City was among the clubs at the center of the emerging East Coast punk scene in the 1970s. *(Flora Carnevale)*

The well-known trapeze artist Karl Wallenda of the Flying Wallendas died in 1978 after falling off a tightrope between two hotels in San Juan, Puerto Rico.

Blue Grass, Blues), featured bands such as Television and the Ramones. Located in a then-rundown neighborhood on the Bowery, CBGB and other downtown clubs such as Max's Kansas City and the Mercer Arts Center started attracting a scene of like-minded disenfranchised folks who found a sense of community outside of society's mainstream.

Punk's importance reverberated throughout American culture. The commercial mainstream finally incorporated punk style, and its influence percolated through fashion, advertising, and art. Eventually punk anthems were used to sell all manner of consumer products, and its appeal spread to the masses, but at the end of the 1970s the music and fashions that accompanied the punk movement were still evidence of outsider status and culture.

CHAPTER 7

THE 1970s
WIND DOWN, 1979

PERRY POWER PLANT

Accident Free Since 2/05/00	Power Level	%
Availability (%)	91.6	
Dose (m-rem)	345227	■
Power Production Cost (¢/kw)	1.23	
Human Performance Success Days	27	

THREE MILE ISLAND, LOCATED IN THE Susquehanna River near Harrisburg, Pennsylvania, was the site of a serious accident that occurred on March 28, 1979. The island housed the Three Mile Island Nuclear Generating Station, and when one of its reactors suffered a malfunction, the emergency cooling systems failed, leading to a partial melting of the station's uranium core and production of hydrogen gas. Thousands living near the plant, fearing a radioactive explosion, left the area before the twelve-day crisis ended.

The towers of nuclear reactors, like these in Perry, Ohio, became a familiar and somewhat frightening image to many Americans after the partial meltdown of a reactor core at Three Mile Island, Pennsylvania. (*AP/Wide World*)

President Carter meets with leaders of an antinuclear rally in Washington, D.C. (*AP/Wide World*)

During the crisis, some radioactive water and gases were released. A federal investigation assigned blame to human, mechanical, and design errors in the plant itself. The investigation recommended many changes at nuclear power plants, as well as in the structure and function of the Nuclear Regulatory Commission (NRC). The NRC, an independent U.S. government commission founded in 1974, is charged with licensing and regulating civilian use of nuclear energy to protect the public and the environment. The accident increased public concern over the dangers of nuclear power and slowed construction of other reactors.

Former U.S. attorney general John N. Mitchell was released on parole in 1979 after serving 19 months at a federal prison in Alabama for his role in the Watergate cover-up.

THE CHINA SYNDROME

The accident at Three Mile Island Nuclear Generating Station occurred just a few days after the release of the movie *The China Syndrome*. In the movie, the lead character is a television anchor, played by Jane Fonda, producing a series on nuclear energy. While she and her cameraman are at a nuclear plant, an accident almost happens. The anchor is inspired to raise public awareness of the plant's dangers. During one scene, she talks to a nuclear safety expert who claims that a meltdown could force an area "the size of Pennsylvania" to be evacuated. The film was nominated for four Academy Awards, including Best Actress (Fonda) and Best Actor (Jack Lemmon).

CHINA INVADES VIETNAM

When Deng Xiaoping went to Washington, D.C., in January 1979 to cement the normalization of China's relations with the United States, he told President Jimmy Carter that China was about to send troops into Vietnam. Not only did Beijing feel Vietnam was acting ungratefully after all the assistance it had received during its war against the United States, but in 1978, the Vietnamese government had begun expelling Vietnamese citizens of Chinese descent. Worst of all, Vietnam was becoming friendlier with the Soviet Union, which the Chinese felt posed a threat.

The Chinese government in Peking (now Beijing) claimed the Vietnamese had made more than 700 armed incursions into China and killed or wounded more than 300 Chinese soldiers and civilians during the previous last six months. With this justification, they sent troops across the China-Vietnam border.

Upon invasion, the Chinese troops were decimated. The Vietnamese cut down the Chinese fighters with machine guns, mines, and booby traps. China withdrew its troops after 17 days, after experiencing heavy casualties. "We do not want a single inch of Vietnamese territory. All we want is a peaceful and stable border, " was he official statement of the Chinese news agency.

On his visit to the United States, Deng Xiaoping signed U.S.-China cooperation agreements on science and technology, culture, education, commerce, and space exploration. Here, he visits NASA. (*NASA*)

Many observers compared the Chinese invasion to U.S. involvement in the Vietnam War; although the situations were very much different, in both cases large and powerful nations were unable to militarily dominate the much smaller nation of Vietnam.

No identifiable injuries due to radiation occurred. However, following the incident, many people, including government officials, worried that cancer rates in the area might go up. The accident also furthered a serious decline in the public popularity of nuclear power. By coincidence, the event occurred just days after the release of the movie *The China Syndrome*, which portrayed a similar, yet fictional, incident.

TOUGH TIMES AT HOME

On June 30, 1979, while on the way home from an economic summit in Tokyo, President Carter received a phone call from a staff member, urging him to return to

Pope John Paul II made a historic visit to the United States in 1979. Although Carter was not a Roman Catholic, he warmly welcomed the pope. Carter met with spiritual leaders of all denominations, and spoke often of faith in his own speeches. (*AP/Wide World*)

the United States right away. That week, the energy crisis that Carter had kept at bay finally erupted. OPEC announced more oil price increases that were bound to send gasoline prices skyrocketing and lead to severe shortages. It was inevitable: As it had during the oil shortage of 1973–1974, long gas-pump lines were bound to form, and with them, flaring tempers and fights.

Americans expressed outrage over the continuing economic decline. Much of that anger was directed at the White House: Carter's approval rating had dropped to 25 percent, lower than Richard Nixon's during the Watergate scandal. The president retreated to Camp David, where he started working on what would be his fifth major speech on energy. Carter soon realized that Americans had stopped listening to him. Instead, he brought in advisers to talk about what could be done, and perhaps find a solution to the nation's malaise. These advisers included members of Congress, governors, labor leaders, academics, and clergy.

AMERICA'S CRISIS OF CONFIDENCE

It seemed that after fifteen years filled with assassinations, Vietnam, Watergate, and a declining economy,

Americans were suffering from a general crisis of confidence. Carter attempted to address the problems and inspire the country to overcome them, but it would prove difficult to regain his popularity and turn his presidency around.

On the evening of July 15, 1979, Americans turned on their televisions to watch Jimmy Carter address the nation in what was to be the most important speech of his presidency.

"I invited to Camp David people from almost every segment of our society—business and labor, teachers and preachers, governors, mayors, and private citizens," said the president. "And then I left Camp David to listen to other Americans, men and women like you," the president told the nation.

First, Carter shared some of the criticism he had received at the domestic summit at Camp David. "This from a southern governor: 'Mr. President, you are not leading this nation—you're just managing the government.'

"This from a young woman in Pennsylvania: 'I feel so far from government. I feel like ordinary people are excluded from political power.'

"We were all saying the same thing: 'You have no idea how bad it is here.'"

—Patrick Caddell, a pollster for President Carter, on the economic crisis and gas shortage of 1979

President Carter visits Bardstown, Kentucky, and climbs out of his car to shake hands on the way to a town meeting in July 1979. Faced with a crisis of confidence in the nation, Carter tried to engage ordinary Americans in dialogue through such meetings. (*AP Photo/Bob Daugherty*)

Cars line up for gas as rationing takes effect. Americans were unused to such measures, and many tried to get around the regulations. (*Library of Congress*)

"And I like this one particularly from a black woman who happens to be the mayor of a small Mississippi town: 'The big-shots are not the only ones who are important. Remember, you can't sell anything on Wall Street unless someone digs it up somewhere else first.'"

The president went on to say that he believed that the solution to the energy crisis could also help conquer the crisis of the spirit in the country. He asked Americans to join him in adapting to a new age of limits, where Americans would have to conserve resources. One of the measures to conserve energy that was implemented in 1979 was gas rationing. In many parts of the country, gas would be sold to people with license plates that ended in either odd, or even numbers, on alternating days.

During the speech, Carter did admit that that some of this crisis of confidence was caused by government inaction and inability to address the growing problems facing America in the 1970s. Carter concluded with a desperate call for a renewal of confidence:

"We simply must have faith in each other. Faith in our ability to govern ourselves and faith in the future of this nation. Restoring that faith and that confidence to America is now the most important task we face."

ANDREW YOUNG

Andrew Young was one of the most high-profile African-American leaders of the 1970s. In 1972, he became Georgia's first African-American congressman since the Reconstruction period that had followed the Civil War. He was re-elected in 1974 and 1976.

In 1976, President Carter appointed Young the U.S. Ambassador to the United Nations. Young held that post until 1979 when, contrary to the policy of the Carter administration, he met with a representative of the Palestinian Liberation Organization (PLO). The PLO denied that Israel, an ally of the United States, had any right to exist and engaged in terrorism to further its political aims.

When it was revealed that the meeting occurred, Young made statements that were perceived as evasive, and he was forced to resign. When President Carter had taken office in the wake of Watergate, he committed his administration to the highest standards of honesty in its public statements. Young's behavior was contrary to those ideals and standards.

Young was elected mayor of Atlanta in 1981 and 1985.

Andrew Young, one of the most prominent African Americans in Carter's administration, resigned after a controversial meeting with the PLO. (*Library of Congress*)

"That was not a lie, it was just not the whole truth."

—U.N. Ambassador Andrew Young, on disclosing an unauthorized meeting with the Palestine Liberation Organization that resulted in Young's resignation

The president also took Americans to task. Confronting the ethos of the "Me decade," he stated that "too many of us now tend to worship self-indulgence and consumption. Human identity is no longer defined by what one does but by what one owns."

Hendrik Hertzberg, who worked on the speech, admits that it "was more like a sermon than a political speech." It became known as Carter's *malaise* speech.

AMERICA'S REACTION

In the days following the television address, the president's approval ratings went up. But then, as historian Douglas Brinkley noted:

> It boomeranged on him. The op-ed pieces started spinning out, "Why don't you fix something? There's nothing wrong with the American people. We're a great people. Maybe the problem's in the White House, maybe we need new leadership to guide us."
>
> But Carter doesn't give Americans any real reasons why they should now have confidence in their government and society. He has reminded Americans of our greatness in the past, but has offered no real program to return America to that greatness and confidence in ourselves in the future.

Faced with negative reactions to the speech, Carter only added fuel to the fire of criticism when he tried to start fresh by conducting a shakeup of his government. He asked his entire cabinet for their resignations; five cabinet members resigned. "I think the idea was that they were going to firm up the administration, show that there was real change by these personnel changes, and move on," remembers Vice-president Mondale. "But the message the American people got was that we were falling apart."

IRAN HOSTAGE CRISIS

In 1979, President Carter reluctantly allowed the deposed shah of Iran, Mohammad Reza Pahlavi into the United States for political asylum and medical treatment. The shah had been a cold war ally of the United States, who had supported his regime despite allegations of corruption and human rights abuses. He had been exiled from his country following a revolution in which a conservative, anti-American Shiite Muslim cleric, the Ayatollah Ruhollah Khomeini, was appointed ruler. The ayatollah was the political and spiritual leader of the revolution, and he set up a fundamentalist government based on the laws of Islam.

The ayatollah insisted that the United States return the shah to Iran, where he would likely be executed. In November 1979, Khomeini urged the Iranian people to demonstrate for the return of the shah. He also urged attacks on United States and Israeli interests. As a result, a group of approximately 500 Iranian students seized the U.S. embassy in Tehran, Iran's capital, on November 4. The group of students called themselves the Imam's Disciples (*imam* is a title for an Islamic religious leader) and proceeded to take 66 American citizens as hostages.

> *"Americans are the Great Satan, the wounded snake."*
>
> —Ayatollah Khomeini, spiritual leader of the Iranian revolution

The Ayatollah Ruhollah Khomeini was born in Iran on May 17, 1900. Exiled in 1964 for his criticism of the shah, Khomeini returned to lead Iran after the Islamic revolution of 1979. *(AP/Wide World)*

President Carter's strongly worded diplomatic letter to the Ayatollah Khomeini requesting release of the hostages fell on deaf ears. His emissaries, Ramsey Clark and William Miller, were unable to negotiate successfully. (*National Archives*)

THE WHITE HOUSE

WASHINGTON

November 6, 1979

Dear Ayatollah Khomeini:

Based on the willingness of the Revolutionary Council to receive them, I am asking two distinguished Americans, Mr. Ramsey Clark and Mr. William G. Miller, to carry this letter to you and to discuss with you and your designees the situation in Tehran and the full range of current issues between the U.S. and Iran.

In the name of the American people, I ask that you release unharmed all Americans presently detained in Iran and those held with them and allow them to leave your country safely and without delay. I ask you to recognize the compelling humanitarian reasons, firmly based in international law, for doing so.

I have asked both men to meet with you and to hear from you your perspective on events in Iran and the problems which have arisen between our two countries. The people of the United States desire to have relations with Iran based upon equality, mutual respect, and friendship.

They will report to me immediately upon their return.

Sincerely,

Jimmy Carter

His Excellency
Ayatollah Khomeini
Qom, Iran

DECLASSIFIED
NSC 4/22/85 re MC-84-10
BY ALTE NARS. DATE 4/29/85

Iranian students pray outside the American embassy, where they held 50 Americans hostage. *(AP/Wide World)*

During the confusion, six Americans escaped and fled to the Canadian embassy in Tehran, where they were given fake Canadian passports. With the false papers, they were able to leave without being identified as Americans. Thirteen more of the hostages were released later in November; these were the women and African Americans in the group. Many months later, another hostage was released because of illness.

Over a period of 444 days, the ayatollah's government held the Americans hostage, and demanded that the shah be returned to Iran to stand trial. The effect on the United States was profound. Never before had so large a group of Americans been held captive by a foreign power during peacetime. Many Americans feared that the hostages were being tortured and would eventually be executed. The Iran hostage crisis was the defining event of the end of the 1970s. For well over a year, Americans watched on their televisions as the blindfolded hostages were exhibited to hostile crowds and television cameras. The hostage crisis contributed directly to President Carter's loss of the 1980 presidential election to Ronald Reagan.

For Iranians involved in the embassy takeover, seizing the hostages was a means of retaliation against

Nine years after the May 4, 1970, Kent State shootings, the state of Ohio agreed to pay $675,000 to families of dead and injured in the incident.

An Iranian woman, one of the students who participated in the embassy hostage crisis, speaks before thousands of Iranians in 1979. The crisis gave new energy and encouragement to religious Islamic leadership in Iran. (*AP/Wide World*)

the United States for its long support of the shah's totalitarian rule. Under the Ayatollah Khomeini, the new Iranian government showed that it would not hesitate, nor was it scared, to stand up to the United States. Such a challenge shook American confidence to the core.

The ayatollah was viciously anti-American, denouncing the American government as "enemies of Islam" and worse. Most U.S. citizens were at first bewildered and then deeply angered by such verbal attacks. An outpouring of national rage led to anti-Khomeini posters, political cartoons, T-shirts, bumper stickers, and even dartboards featuring the image of the Ayatollah Khomeini. Others focused their energy on getting the hostages home safely. One symbol of solidarity was a yellow ribbon tied around a tree, meant to remain there as a public reminder until the hostages were freed. In some neighborhoods, nearly every home had a yellow ribbon tied around a tree on the lawn.

CARTER ACTS

President Carter moved rapidly to apply economic and diplomatic pressure on Iran. The United States stopped importing oil from Iran almost immediately, some Iranian nationals in the U.S. were expelled, and on November 14, 1979, billions of dollars of Iranian assets in the U.S. were frozen so that Iranian companies could not conduct business. Carter pledged himself to preserving the lives of the hostages, but beyond these initial measures he could do little.

The Iranian government issued a set of demands in return for freeing the hostages. They demanded the

SALT II

President Carter enjoyed several successes in foreign policy. One such achievement was the Strategic Arms Limitations Talks (SALT II) with Soviet premier Leonid Brezhnev in Vienna, Austria. The goal of the talks was to curtail the manufacture of strategic nuclear weapons. It was a continuation of progress made during the SALT I talks, which had resulted in the two nations signing an Anti-Ballistic Missile Treaty on May 26, 1972. An agreement to limit strategic nuclear weapons launchers was reached in Vienna on June 18, 1979, and was signed by Soviet leader Leonid Brezhnev and President Carter.

President Carter and Soviet premier Leonid Brezhnev celebrate the signing of the SALT II treaty. (*AP/Wide World*)

> **The Sugar Hill Gang released the first commercial rap hit, "Rapper's Delight," in 1979, bringing rap off the New York streets and into the popular music scene.**

return of the shah to Iran and certain diplomatic moves, including an apology for prior American actions in Iran and a promise to not to interfere in the future. Carter rejected these demands, but it seemed that the U.S. government did not have a clear idea how to secure the safe release of its captive citizens. As the decade drew to a close, the Carter administration appeared to much of the American public as ineffectual and beset by uncertainty.

SHADES OF THINGS TO COME: VIDEO GAMES AND HIP-HOP

Though video games had been a popular staple in arcades and on early home systems since the arrival of the game Pong earlier in the decade, it was the release of the game Space Invaders that made playing these games spiral into one of the most popular recreational activities in the United States. Space Invaders was originally made in Japan, and in 1978, an American company, Midway

THE ATARI GAME SYSTEM

The Atari game system started a revolution in home entertainment. The consoles and joysticks available in the 1970s were nowhere near as sophisticated as the game systems that followed, but Atari developed several products and game consoles that captured and held consumers' attention throughout the decade.

Pong, the first game available for Atari home systems, was monochrome; it featured only one color, like early computer monitors. Later versions used more than one color, and sales skyrocketed. The Atari games were often simplified ver-

An Atari joystick was essential for any serious video game player. (*National Archives*)

sions of games found in video arcades. When Space Invaders, a hugely popular arcade game, became available for Atari systems, sales really took off.

The popularity of home video game systems helped the development of software and hardware that led to greater sophistication in home computer systems, as well. In fact, Steve Jobs, the founder of Apple Computer, once worked at Atari. Atari itself produced and sold many home computer systems derived from the company's video game console development and its employees' expertise.

Manufacturing, gained the license to produce it in the United States. Space Invaders was a futuristic take on a shooting gallery game, featuring lines of evil aliens steadily advancing on the player. Simplistic in comparison to the games that would appear just a few years later, it nonetheless had a tremendous impact. By the end of 1979, countless Americans could be found spending their leisure time in arcades, pumping quarter after quarter into a Space Invaders game.

Though primitive when compared to the consoles available in the decades to come, home video game systems, such as Atari 2600, also became popular at the end of the decade. By the early 1980s, new video games in a variety of styles had flooded the market, and the craze had become big business.

The origins of hip-hop culture and its associated art forms came about during the late 1970s. Graffiti

Graffiti bloomed on New York City subway cars throughout the 1970s. Very few of the cars on the 232-mile subway system were free of graffiti. (*National Archives*)

"I said a hip, hop, the hippie to the hippie to the hip hip hop, a you don't stop the rock it to the bang bang boogie, say up jumped the boogie to the rhythm of the boogie, the beat."

—*Rapper's Delight* by the Sugar Hill Gang, 1979

had become widespread in urban areas during the decade. In New York City, subway cars were all but completely covered with a variety of often indecipherable words and images. Much graffiti consisted of the tags, or names of the people wielding the spray cans, and taggers developed their own intricate rivalries and status system. Many considered tagging an unsightly form of vandalism, but there also were many intricately painted murals, often appearing on playground walls and the sides of subway cars. Known as burners, these large-scale pieces featured stylized script and colorful graphics and were viewed as art by a number of people.

Break-dancing began in the Bronx, New York, but spread quickly through inner-city urban areas. The children here, in Lawrence, Massachusetts, practice their moves in front of a graffiti wall mural. (*AP/Wide World*)

Along with graffiti and the athletic dance form known as break-dancing, another element of hip-hop was rap music. Through the early years of the decade, inner city neighborhoods in the Bronx, New York, for example, had hosted street parties featuring large sound systems manned by DJs, who played records, and MCs, who talked over the music, provoking the audience or encouraging them to dance. As MCs started to tell stories and boast in rhyme, the skill of rapping emerged. Rejecting the polished, commercial sound of disco, but maintaining the heavy, percussive beat, DJs would mix records together with two turntables, often scratching the records back and forth to accentuate the rhythm, and concentrated on the break beats between verses of a particular song. In turn, the MCs would rhyme over the break, and this eventually became an integral part of the music. Rap music had become increasingly popular in urban areas by 1979.

Early rap recordings featured backing instrumental tracks from popular hits of the day, with crews of rappers intoning over the music. Using the music from Chic's number one hit *Good Times,* New York's Sugarhill Gang became the first rap group to achieve a gold record, selling more than 500,000 copies of their single *Rapper's Delight* in 1979. Rap music would not fully break through as a popular form of commercial mainstream music until a few years later, but its audience was steadily growing.

THE MORAL MAJORITY

There is no doubt that many challenges faces the United States during the late 1970s—a stagnant economy, growing inflation, and rising prices on foreign oil imports. Economic pressure on traditional, single-income families grew. Social changes, such as higher divorce rates, feminism, and gay rights affected family structure as well. Americans were deeply divided in their

A legend in his heyday with the Detroit Red Wings, Gordie Howe returned to the NHL in 1979 following its merger with the upstart WHA. Before finally retiring at age 52, the grandfather scored 15 goals for the Hartford Whalers, briefly skating with his sons.

The first gay rights march in the United States took place in Washington, D.C., on October 14, 1979, with an estimated 100,000 people attending.

> *"...the art of politics is to be ahead of your time—about six months will do it. Any more than that, and people forget you were there."*
>
> —Feminist Gloria Steinem, 1979

feelings about these issues. At Carter's White House Conference on Families, conservative Christians chose to polarize themselves from the existing political parties of the Democrats and Republicans. While conservatives had existed in the Republican Party for decades, another branch of conservatism emerged in the late 1970s—the New Right.

The New Right shared certain beliefs about the power structure in the United States. They used the term *Eastern establishment* to refer to social and political elite in Boston, New York, and Washington, many of whom had attended Ivy League universities. These Republicans were seen as wealthy liberals who did not represent the majority of the Republican Party. A remarkable development in the rise of the New Right, however, was the emergence of the Christian Right. Religious Christian conservatives had been involved in politics for generations, but now new issues, such as *Roe v. Wade,* legalizing abortion, energized them. These groups experienced an almost overnight success, registering millions of evangelical Christian voters and influencing the outcome of local and even national Congressional elections in the late 1970s.

Jerry Falwell, the leader of the Moral Majority, attracted much publicity. Here he rides a steer at a Republican fundraiser in Texas. (*AP/Wide World*)

PHYLLIS SCHLAFLY

Phyllis Schlafly gained prominence as part of the Stop ERA movement early in the 1970s. Although she was perceived as an opponent of feminism, her own career was marked by achievement in the traditionally male world of conservative politics. By the end of the decade, she herself had gained a place as one of the few women leaders in the Moral Majority movement.

Phyllis Schlafy popularized an anti-feminist stance. (*AP/Wide World*)

Chief among the leaders of this movement were Pat Robertson and Reverend Jerry Falwell, who called his group the Moral Majority. Opponents of his group used the saying, "The Moral Majority is neither," meaning that the Moral Majority was neither moral nor a majority. While Christians on the right brought energy, large television and radio audiences, and renewed patriotism to the New Right, much of the Christian Right's position was based on a moral view about social issues.

Another high profile leader of the Christian Right was Phyllis Schlafly, who had vigorously and vocally opposed the Equal Rights Amendment on the grounds that it would bring about a "gender-free society." Other leaders spoke out against women's rights and gay rights.

SHAPES OF THINGS TO COME

Though the decade of the 1970s seemed quiet at times, it was the culmination of themes introduced in the 60s, and foreshadowed major changes in American life to come. These themes would continue to grow in importance throughout the rest of the 20th century, marking

Skylab, **America's first space station, which had been orbiting earth since 1973, plunged to Earth six years later, scattering debris across the southern Indian Ocean and sparsely populated Western Australia.**

U.S. politics and dividing American society into increasingly vocal and disparate groups. Identity politics, the struggle between liberals and conservatives, and American interests in the Middle East were all in the forefront and on the front pages by the end of the 1970s, replacing the hippies, drug culture, and furor over the Vietnam War that had marked the beginning of the decade.

Despite the opinion of some, the 1970s were not a decade in which nothing happened. The roots of eco-

FOUND IN SPACE

When the Skylab station experiment ended in 1979, scientists had gained a huge amount of knowledge about how the human body functions in space. *Skylab* was designed to be lived in for a month or more at a time. It was a home as well as a spaceship. Since its launch in May 1973, the station orbited Earth hundreds of times, and three different teams of astronauts had lived aboard the station for 28, 59, and 84 days.

Astronauts woke at 6 A.M. and went to bed at 10 P.M. They performed medical experiments on each other, maintained the station, did housekeeping, and conducted all kinds of scientific experiments. The major feature of the Skylab life was microgravity, or an almost complete lack of gravity. Astronauts and objects floated freely throughout the station unless securely fastened.

Some of the experiments were not so scientific; one astronaut smuggled a tape of his wife's voice aboard, then played it back to Mission Control on Earth. The bewildered Mission Control listeners heard Helen, astronaut Owen Garriot's wife, say, "The boys hadn't had a home-cooked meal in so long I thought I'd just bring one up." Others experimented with watching blobs of water float through the cabin. One of their favorite activities was looking back down on Earth.

Unlike previous astronauts, who had to squeeze meals out of a tube, Skylab staff could select their own menu and heat it up as they liked. (*NASA*)

nomic recovery and the computer revolution, the rise of Republican conservatism, and questions about America' role on the world stage that marked the 1980s and beyond can all be found in the 1970s. As the decade came to a close, turmoil still plagued U.S. society. Though the cynicism and mistrust of the Watergate era had receded, an aura of doubt and uncertainty had emerged in the American psyche, as the continuing hostage crisis in Iran and worries about the economy and the Carter presidency remained at the forefront of peoples' concern. A sense of skepticism and a more pronounced tendency to question prevalent values, whether of established lifestyles, or the government itself, had taken hold among the American people.

Despite predictions of doom, *Skylab*'s disintegration upon falling back to Earth had no ill effects; no cities were destroyed, nor were people killed. (*NASA*)

GLOSSARY

Affirmative Action System designed to remedy past discrimination, implemented to ensure that individuals have equal opportunity without regard to their race, sex, or ethnicity.

AIM (American Indian Movement) A Native American civil rights group that led a number of demonstrations and protests in the 1970s.

bicentennial celebration Festivities on July 4, 1976, surrounding the 200th anniversary of the signing of the Declaration of Independence.

biotechnology The use of biological processes or living organisms to manufacture products.

Blaxploitation Combines the words "black" and "exploitation"; refers mainly to stylized, sensational, low-budget films in the 1970s which featured mostly African-American casts and directors.

détente French term meaning the relaxation of tensions. It refers to a policy of improved relations between the United States and the Soviet Union during the 1970s.

disco Popular dance music of the late 1970s.

domino theory A concept held by some U.S. politicians during the cold war, asserting that if one nation in a region fell under communist control, then other neighboring countries would follow suit, like a row of dominoes.

dove A pacifist. During the 1970s, it referred to those who opposed U.S. military involvement in Vietnam.

energy crisis The shortage, and accompanying rise in price, of oil, electricity, and fossil fuels.

ERA (Equal Rights Amendment) Proposed amendment to the U.S. Constitution that stated "equality of rights under the law shall not be denied or abridged by the United States or by any State on account of sex."

fad A brief craze. A fad usually enjoys massive popularity before fading quickly.

feminism Political and social movement aimed at securing equal rights for women.

hawk A person who favors war or a warlike attitude as national policy. During the 1970s, it referred to those who supported U.S. military involvement in Vietnam.

hot pants Skin-tight, very short pants.

identity politics Political positions that focus on the concerns of specific social groups identified by gender, race, ethnicity, or sexual orientation.

inflation   Increase in the cost of goods and services, and/or a decline in the purchasing power of money.

Khmer Rouge   Communist regime that ruled Cambodia, 1975–1979.

"Me" decade   A popular term describing the 1970s. It referred to the assumption that in the 1970s, people concentrated on the individual pursuit of leisure and personal happiness, rather than addressing the ills of society through rebellion and protest.

miniskirt   A very short skirt.

Moral Majority   Group founded by Reverend Jerry Falwell in 1979 to organize conservative Christians into a powerful voting bloc and push for laws reflecting their values.

Ms.   Title used with a woman's last name. Unlike traditional titles of *Miss* and *Mrs.*, it does not refer to marital status. Also the name of the first feminist magazine, founded in 1971.

OPEC (Organization of Petroleum Exporting Countries)   International organization comprised mainly of Arab countries in the Middle East.

POSSLQ (Persons of the Opposite Sex Sharing Living Quarters)   This term was coined in the late 1970s by the U.S. Census Bureau.

punk   A type of loud, aggressive rock music. Punk rejected the conformity of popular culture and promoted a "do-it-yourself" mentality. Its social and political beliefs were reflected in music, ideology, and fashion.

recession   A cycle of reduced economic growth, marked by a rise in unemployment and inflation.

SALT (Strategic Arms Limitations Talks)   Negotiations between the United States and the Soviet Union to limit both countries' nuclear weapons.

stagflation   Twin economic problems of stagnation and inflation, in which the nation's economy was characterized by relatively high price inflation and low (or negative) rates of economic growth.

Vietnamization   President Nixon's policy to bring about the U.S. military's gradual disengagement from the war in Vietnam.

Watergate   Scandal that led to Nixon's resignation in 1974. It was discovered the Republican White House had planned and covered up a burglary at Democratic Party headquarters, which was located at the Watergate Hotel.

women's liberation   Movement organized around a belief in the social, political, and economic equality of the sexes.

FURTHER READING

BOOKS

Bailey, Beth and David Farber, eds. *America in the Seventies*. Lawrence: University Press of Kansas, 2004.

Biskind, Peter. *Easy Riders, Raging Bulls: How the Sex-Drugs-And-Rock-N-Roll Generation Saved Hollywood*. New York: Simon & Schuster, 1998.

Brownmiller, Susan. *In Our Time: Memoir of Revolution*. New York: The Dial Press, 1999.

Carroll, Peter. *It Seemed Like Nothing Happened: America in the 1970s*. Piscataway, N.J.: Rutgers University Press, 1990.

David, Kenneth C. *Don't Know Much About American History*. New York: Harper Collins, 2003.

Feinstein, Stephen. *The 1970s: From Watergate to Disco*. Berkeley Heights, N.J.: Enslow Publishers, 2000.

Frum, David. *How We Got Here: The 70's—The Decade that Brought You Modern Life—For Better or Worse*. New York: Basic Books, 1999.

Kahn, Ashley, George-Warren Holly, and Shawn Dahl, eds. *Rolling Stone: The Seventies*. New York: Little, Brown & Company, 1998.

Katz, William Loren. *The Great Society to the Reagan Era, 1964–1990*. Austin, Tex.: Raintree Steck-Vaughn, 1993.

Lader, Curt. *Painless American History*. New York: Barrons, 1999.

Olson, James S., ed. *Historical Dictionary of the 1970s*. Westport, Conn.: Greenwood Press, 1999.

Pluto, Terry. *Loose Balls: The Short, Wild Life of the American Basketball Association*. New York: Simon & Schuster. 1990

Schulman, Bruce J. *The Seventies: The Great Shift in American Culture, Society and Politics*. New York: The Free Press, 2001.

Smith, Paul Chaat, and Robert Allen Warrior. *Like a Hurricane: The Indian Movement from Alcatraz to Wounded Knee*. New York: The New Press. 1996.

Stewart, Gail. *The 1970s*. Cultural History of the United States Through the Decades. San Diego, Calif.: Lucent Books, 1999

WEB SITES

"Ask Mr. Pop History," Available online. URL: http://www.pophistorynow.com/index.htm/. Downloaded in June 2005.

Associated Press. *A pardon to end 'an American tragedy.'* Houston Chronicle Interactive. Available online. URL: http://www.chron.com/content/interactive/special/watergate/pardon.html. Posted on June 7, 1997. Downloaded in August 2005.

Barry, John W. Donors and the Decade of Disco: *Looking back unfondly on the 1970s*. The Philanthropy Roundtable. Available online. URL: http://www.philanthropyroundtable.org/magazines/2000-05/barry.html. Posted in May 2000.

Bellis, Mary. *20th Century Inventions 1951–1975*. Available online. URL: http://inventors.about.com/library/weekly/aa122999a.htm. Downloaded in August 2005.

"Carter, Jimmy," Available online. URL: http://en.wikipedia.org/wiki/Jimmy_Carter/. Downloaded in June 2005.

Christensen, John. *Echoes of War: Vietnam: The War That Won't Go Away*. CNN Interactive, 2001. Available online. URL: http://www.cnn.com/SPECIALS/2000/vietnam/story/America.at.25. Downloaded in August 2005.

DeLong, Brad. *The Inflation of the 1970s*. University of California at Berkeley and National Bureau of Economic Research. Available online. URL: http://econ161.berkeley.edu/Econ_Articles/theinflationofthes.html. Downloaded in August 2005.

Dirks, Tim. *Film History of the 1970s.* Available online. URL: http://www.filmsite.org/70sintro.html. Updated 2005.

"Energy Crisis," Available online. URL: http://en.wikipedia.org/wiki/Energy_crisis/. Downloaded in June 2005.

"Fads of the 1970s," Available online. URL: http://www.crazyfads.com/70s.htm/. Downloaded in June 2005.

Gillis, Charles. *American Cultural History, 1970–1979.* Kingwood College Library, 1999. Available online. URL: http://kclibrary.nhmccd.edu/decade70.html. Downloaded in June 2005.

Herbers, John. *On This Day: The 37th President— In Three Decades.* The New York Times Online: April 24, 1994. Available online. URL: http://www.nytimes.com/learning/general/onthisday/bday/0109.html. Downloaded in August 2005.

"Mood Ring," Available online. URL: http://www.super70s.com/Super70s/Culture/Fads/Mood_Ring.asp/. Downloaded in June 2005.

OakRidge National Laboratory. *The Seventies: Energy Urgency.* Available online. URL: http://www.ornl.gov/info/swords/seventies.html. Downloaded in August 2005.

Polasky, Rod. Archeolink: *1970s America.* Available online. URL: http://www.archeolink.com/1970s_united_states_history.htm#1970s. Downloaded October 2005.

President Ford's Speech on the Fall of Vietnam, 24 April 1975. Available online. URL: http://www.vietnamwar.net/Ford-1.htm. Downloaded in August 2005.

"Seventies, The: Year by Year," Available online. URL: http://www.nostalgiacentral.com/. Downloaded in June 2005.

Sullivan, Terry. *Prelude: Searching for a Framework.* Available online. URL: http://www.ibiblio.org/sullivan/CampDavid-Prelude.html. Downloaded in June 2005.

Tuchman, Gary. *Kent State forever linked with Vietnam War era.* Available online. URL: http://www.cnn.com/SPECIALS/views/y/2000/04/tuchman.kentstate.may4/index.html. Downloaded in August 2005.

Public Broadcasting Service (PBS), WGBH Educational Foundation. *American Experience: Nixon's China Game.* Available online. URL: http://www.pbs.org/wgbh/amex/china/index.html. Downloaded in June 2005.

White House Presidential Biographies. Richard M. Nixon: Available online. URL: http://www.whitehouse.gov/history/presidents/rn37.html. Gerald R. Ford: Available online. URL: http://www.whitehouse.gov/history/presidents/gf38.html. Jimmy Carter: Available online. URL: http://www.whitehouse.gov/history/presidents/jc39.html. Downloaded in August 2005.

VH1. *I Love the '70s.* Available online. URL: http://www.vh1.com/shows/dyn/i_love_the_70s/series.jhtml. Downloaded October 2005.

INDEX

Page numbers in *italics* indicate illustrations. Page numbers followed by *g* indicate glossary entries. Page numbers in **boldface** indicate box features.

A

Aaron, Hank 56
abortion 26–27, 91, 116
Abzug, Bella *15*
Affirmative Action 33–34, 120*g*
African Americans
    14–15, 33–34, 59, **105**. *See also*
    civil rights
    Black Power 16
    major league admittance 56
    music 94
    politicans 5, 6
    unemployment 33, 62
    women 5, 6, 14, *27*
Agnew, Spiro T. 11, 39, *40*–41
Air Force One 25, 51
Algeria 30
Ali, Muhammad **50**, **51**
All in the Family (television show) **11**
All the President's Men (Woodward and Bernstein) 36
Allegheny Airlines **19**
Allen, Irwin 54
Allen, Woody 54
Ambrose, Stephen 8
American Automobile Association (AAA) 31
American Ballet Theatre 45
American Basketball Association (ABA) 69–70
American Broadcasting Company (ABC) 52, 53
American Football League (AFL) 14
American Freedom Train 59
American Indian Movement (AIM) 16–17, **49**, 120*g*
American Indians 14
Amnesty International **51**
Animal House (film) 53, **84**
answering machine 46
Anti-Ballistic Missile Treaty (1972) **111**
antiwar protests 5, 7, 8
Apocalypse Now (film) 86
Apollo-Soyuz spacecraft 47
Apollo space mission 18, 19
Apple computers *92*

Arber, Werner 93
Army, U.S. 7
Atari **112**, 113
Atlanta Braves **56**
Atlanta, Georgia 59
automatic teller machines (ATMs) 66
Ayatollah Khomeini 74, 107–112
Aykroyd, Dan 53

B

Bakke, Allan 88
Banks, Dennis 16
Barnes, Marvin 70
Baryshnikov, Mikhail 43
baseball 29, 56, 69, 84–85
basketball 69–71
Battle of the Sexes 31–32
Beale, Howard 62
Beatles, The 55
Bee Gees 94
Begin, Menachem 76–79
Belushi, John 53
Bernstein, Carl 35
Berra, Yogi 29
Betamax 46
Bicentennial celebration **61**, 120*g*
Bill of Rights 61
Billy Beer **75**
biotechnology 91–93, 120*g*
Black Caesar (film) **15**
Black Panther Party 16
Black Power 16
Blacula (film) **15**
blaxploitation **15**, 120*g*
Blue, Vida 29
Blues Brothers, The (film) 53
Books, Mel 27
Boston Women's Health Collective **28**
Bowie, David 55
boxing **50**, 72
break-dancing 114, 115
Bremer, Arthur 22
Brezhnev, Leonid 26, **111**
Brinkley, Douglas 79, 80, 106
Brown, Louise Joy **93**
Bryant, Bobby *69*
bulletin board system (BBS) **92**
Bureau of Indian Affairs (BIA) 17
Burger, Warren E. *26*, 38, *55*

C

Caddell, Patrick 103

calculators 18–19
Calhoun, John 40
Cambodia 47
Camp David summit 75–80
Canfora, Alan 8
Cannon, James 43–44
Captain Fantastic and the Brown Dirt Cowboy (album) 55
Carter, Billy **75**
Carter, Jimmy **49**, 73
    antinuclear rally *100*
    background 59
    Camp David summit 61, 75–80
    crisis of confidence 102–106
    economy 62–64
    election of 1976 57–58, 59
    energy crisis 65–67, 101–102
    family 60
    inauguration 60
    Iran Hostage Crisis 107–112, 119
    malaise speech 106
    Panama Canal Treaty 80–81
    Playboy interview 60
Carter, Rosalynn 60, *76*, 77, 81–82
Casio 18
CBGB 97–98
Central Broadcasting System (CBS) 52
Chase, Chevy 53
Chic 115
Chicago White Sox **95**
China 6
    Open Door Policy 24–25
    Vietnam invasion **101**
China Syndrome, The (film) **100**, 101
Chisholm, Shirley 14, 22
cigarette smoking 18
Cimino, Michael 86
Cincinnati Reds 29
Citizen's Band (CB) Radio **69**
civil rights 13–17, 33–34, 59. *See also* women's liberation
Civil Rights Act (1964) 34–35
Civil Rights Act (1965) 88
Civil War **105**
Clark, Ramsey 108
Clash, The 97
Clay, Cassius. *See* Muhammad Ali
Cleopatra Jones (film) **15**
Cohen, Mark B. 88
cold war 26

colleges and universities 14, 16, 27
Comaneci, Nadia 72
Committee to Re-elect the President (CREEP) 36
Commodore 18
communism 6, 7, 24, 47
computers 18, **92**
Congress, U.S. 5
Congressional Black Caucus 14, 62
Constitution, U.S. 15, 61, 89
Continental Divide (film) 53
Cooper, Alice 55
Coppola, Francis Ford 51, 86
Cosell, Howard **53**
Cotton Comes to Harlem (film) **15**
counter-culture 9, 11
Court, Margaret **32**
Crick, Francis 91
crisis of confidence 102–106
Csonka, Larry 69

D

Dahl, Gary 68
Daily News **49**
Dallas Cowboys 84
Damned, The 97
Daniels, Anthony *86*
De Niro, Robert 54
Dean, John 36
Declaration of Independence **61**
Deep Throat 35
Deer Hunter, The (film) 86
Democratic Kampuchea, 49. *See also* Cambodia
Deng Xiaoping **101**
Denver Nuggets 71
deoxyribonucleic acid (DNA) 91, 93
Department of Energy (1977) 74
détente 6, 120*g*
disco 13, 93–95, 120*g*
discrimination 16, 14. *See also* civil rights
Disney World 11
divorce rates 115
Dole, Robert 42, 55, *59*
domino theory 9, 120*g*
Doors, The 13
doves 9, 120*g*
drug culture 13, 118
Dulles, John Foster 25

E

Eagleton, Thomas **25**

Earth Day 12
Earthquake (film) 55
Eastern establishment 116
ecology flag *12*
Economic Stimulus Appropriations Act (1976) 63–64
economy 5, 11
    during Carter administration 49–50, 59, 62–64, 87
    during Nixon administration 17–18, 33
education 14
Egypt 30, 75
Ehrlichman, John 36
Electric Company, The (television show) 27
Ellsberg, Daniel 20
energy crisis 12, 33, 65–67, 104, 120*g*
environmental movement 12
Equal Employment Opportunity Act (1972) 34
Equal Employment Opportunity Commission (EEOC) 88
Equal Rights Amendment (ERA) 15, 22, 51, 89–91, 117, 120*g*
Erving, Julius 70, 71

F

fads 66, 120*g*
Falwell, Jerry 116, 117
Family Assistance Plan 18
fashion **19**, 68, 94
Federal Bureau of Investigation (FBI) 16, 39
Feinstein, Dianne 89
Felt, Mark 36
feminism 15–16, 115, **117**, 120*g*
Final Days (Woodward and Bernstein) 36
Finch, Peter 62
First Amendment 19, 59
Fisher, Bobby 26
Fisher, Carrie *86*
floppy disk 19
Flying Wallendas 98
football 69, 71, 84
Forbes (magazine) 86
Ford, Betty *38*, *50*, 51, **69**
Ford, Gerald R. *38*, 39, 40, 41, 43–44
    assassination attempts on **46**
    background 43, 51
    economy 49–50
    election of 1976 57, 59

foreign policy 46–47
    media portrayal 51–52
    Nixon's pardon 44–46, 56
Ford, Harrison *86*
Foreman, George **52**
Foster, Jodie 54
Fourteenth Amendment 88
Frazier, Joe **52**
Free to Be You and Me (television show) 27
Frum, David 64

G

Garriot, Owen 118
Gary, Indiana 14
gasoline 31, 66, 102–104
gay rights 115, 117
Gaye, Marvin 13
generation gap 13
Gervin, George 71
Gibb brothers, *94*. *See also* Bee Gees
"Give Peace a Chance" (song) 13
"God Save the Queen" (song) **96**
"gonzo" journalism 36
Goodbye Yellow Brick Road (album) 55
Gordy, Lillian 59, *60*
"Got To Be There" (song) 13
Government as Good as Its People, A (Carter) 56
graffiti 114, 115
Grease (film) **83**
Gretzky, Wayne 70
Grier, Rosie 27
Griffiths, Martha *16*
Guinness, Alec 86

H

Hakuta, Ken 68
Haldeman, H. R. 36
Happy Days (television show) **83**
Harris, Fred 22
hawks 9, 120*g*
Hee Haw (television show) 72
Helsinki Accords 47
Hendrix, Jimi *12*, 13
Herr, Michael 48
Hertzberg, Hendrik 106
Hewlett-Packard 18
Hillman, Darnell 70
Hindenburg, The (film) 55
hip-hop 113–115
hippies 118
Ho Chi Minh City, 47. *See also* Saigon

hockey 69, 71
homosexuals, 14. *See also* gay
    rights
hostage crisis 107–112, 119
hot pants **19**, 120*g*
*How to Create Your Own Fad and
    Make a Million Dollars*
    (Hakuta) 68
How We Got Here: The 1970s
    (Frum) 64
Howe, Gordie 70, 71, 115
Hull, Bobby 69
Humphrey, Hubert 22
Hunter, Catfish 29, 85

I

identity politics 13–14, 120*g*
imam 107
in-vitro fertilization (IVF) **93**
income avergae 5
Indiana Pacers 71
inflation 50, 61, 115, 121*g. See
    also* economy
Intel 19
International Business Machines
    (IBM) 19
Iran 73, 74
    hostage crisis 107–112, 119
Iraq 30
Israel 30–31, 76
Israel-Egypt Peace Treaty 79
"It's Alright to Cry" (song) 27

J

Jackson, Henry (Scoop) 22
Jackson, Jesse 33–34
Jackson, Michael 13
Jackson, Reggie 29, 85
Jaws (film) 86
Jenner, Bruce 72
Jewish Americans 5, 29
John, Elton 55
John Paul II (pope) *102*
Johnson, Lyndon B. 8, 19
Joplin, Janis 13
Jordan 30, 75

K

Kennedy, John F. **25**
Kennedy, Ted **25**
Kent State protest 8, 109
Kerr, Johnny 70
Kerry, John 23
Khmer Rouge 49, 121*g*
King, Billy Jean 31–32

King, Martin Luther, Jr. 59
KISS 55–56
Kiss Army 56
Kissinger, Henry A. 24, 45, 46
Knievel, Evel 84
Kuwait 30

L

Laverne and Shirley (television
    show) **83**
Lebanon 30
leisure suits 68
Lennon, John 13
Leonard, Sugar Ray 72
Libya 30
Liddy, G. Gordon 36
Lilies of the Field (film) **15**
Lindsay, John 22
Los Angeles Dodgers 29
Lou Reed and the New York
    Dolls 55
Lucas, George 86
Lucey, Pat **25**
Lydon, John **96**

M

Malone, Moses 71
Mao Zedong 24–25
Marines, U.S. 74
marriage 67
Mars exploration 6, **64**
Marshall, Thurgood 14
Mayhew, Peter *86*
McCall, C. W. **69**
McGovern, George 22, 23, **25**,
    35
McGraw, Tug 29
McLuhan, Marshall 6
Me decade 82–83, 84, 106, 121*g*
Means, Russell 16
Meir, Golda 30
Memphis, Tennessee 84
Messier, Mark 71
Miami Dolphins 69
Michaels, Lorne 52
microprocessor 19
Milk, Harvey 89
Miller, William 108
miniskirt **19**, 121*g*
Minnesota Vikings 69
Mitchell, John N. 36, 100
Mondale, Walter 56, 92, 106
"Monday Night Football"
    (television show) **53**
Mood rings 68

Moon exploration 19
Moore, Sara Jane **46**
Moral Majority 115–117, 121*g*
Morocco 30
Morrison, Jim 13
Moscone, George 89
movies 51–53, 86
Ms. (magazine) 15, **28**, 121*g*
Munich, Germany 28
music 13, 55–56, 68, 93–98,
    113–115
Muskie, Edmund 22

N

Nastase, Ilie 32
Nathans, Daniel 93
Nation of Islam **52**
National Aeronautics and Space
    Administration (NASA) 18,
    19, 64, **101**
National Basketball Association
    (NBA) 70–71
National Black Political
    Convention 14
National Broadcasting Company
    (NBC) 52
National Football League (NFL)
    14
National Forest Service **69**
National Hockey League (NHL)
    69, 71, 115
National Zoo (Washington, D.C.)
    24
Nationalists, Chinese 24
Network (film) 60
Never Mind the Bollocks (album)
    96
New Jersey Nets 71
New York (magazine) **15**
New York Mets 11, 29
New York Nets 70, 71
New York Times v. the United States
    (1971) 19–20
Newsweek (magazine) **84**
Nicaragua 73, 74
Nixon, Richard Milhous
    Cambodia invasion 8
    diplomacy 10, 24–25
    economy 17–18
    inauguration 7
    Israeli aid 30–31
    pardon 44–46, 56
    presidency, first term 6–11
    presidency, second term 21,
        23–26, 30

resignation 37–40, 41
Watergate scandal 35–37, 41, 43, 50, 56
nolo contendere 41
Noriega, Manuel Antonio 81
North Vietnam, 6, 24, 47–48. *See also* Vietnam War
nuclear power plants 67, 99–101
Nuclear Regulatory Commission (NRC) 100

O

Oakland A's 29
oil embargo, 30–31. *See also* gasoline; Organization of Petroleum Exporting Countries (OPEC)
Ojibwa (Annishinabe) Nation 16
Olympics 28–29, **55**, 68, 71–72
O'Neill, Tip *50*
Operation PUSH 33
Operation Sail **61**
Organization of Petroleum Exporting Countries (OPEC) 31, 61, 102, 121*g*
Osbourne, John 42

P

Pahlevi, Reza (shah of Iran) *73*, 74, 107
Palestine Liberation Organization (PLO) 105
Palmer, Laurie 47
Panama Canal 59
Panama Canal Treaty 80–81
"Parents Are People" (song) 27
Paris Peace Talks 24
Peltier, Leonard **51**, *51*
Pentagon Papers 19–20
People United to Save Humanity (PUSH) 33
People's Republic of China. *See* China
Persons of Opposite Sex Sharing Living Quarters (POSSLQ) 67, 121*g*
pesticides 12
Pet Rocks 68
Pine Ridge Reservation 17
Pittsburgh Steelers 84
Playboy (magazine) 60
Poitier, Sidney **15**
Pol Pot 47
Pong 112
Poseidon Adventure, The (film) 54

post–World War II 16
Powell, Lewis F. 88
Presley, Elvis 84
Pryor, Richard 53
Public Health Cigarette Smoking Act (1971) **18**
punk rock 96–98, 121*g*

R

radio **69**
Radner, Gilda 53
Ramadan 30
Ramones, The 97
"Rapper's Delight" (song) 112, 114, 115
Reagan, Ronald 55, 109
recession 63, 121*g*. *See also* economy
Red Power movement 16
Redneck Power (Carter) **75**
Reed, Lou 55
Regents of the University of California v. Bakke (1978) 87, 88
Rehabilitation Act (1973) 35
Reserve Officers Training Corp (ROTC) 8
Reynolds, Joshua 68
Riggs, Bobby 32
Robertson, Pat 117
Rockefeller, John D. 42
Rockefeller, Nelson 39, 41–42
Roe, Jane 26
Roe v. Wade (1973) 26-27, 116
Rolling Stone (magazine) 36
Rotten, Johnny **96**, 97
Russo, Anthony J. 20
rust belt 33
Ruth, Babe **56**

S

Sadat, Anwar-el 75, 76–79
Saigon 47–48
Salinger, Pierre **25**
SALT (Strategic Arms Limitation Talks) 121*g*
same-sex marriage 91
San Antonio Spurs 71
Saturday Night Fever (film) 95
Saturday Night Live (television show) 51, 52–53, 68, **84**
Saudi Arabia 30
Schlafly, Phyllis 90–91, **117**
science 18–19
Scorsese, Martin 53

Sears Tower 30
Seaver, Tom 11
Senate, U.S. 15
Sesame Street (television show) 27
Sex Pistols **96**, 97
Sha Na Na **83**
Shaft (film) **15**
Sihanouk, Norodom *48*
Silent Majority 7, 10
Simmons, Gene *56*
Singer, Isaac Bashevis 91
Six Day War of 1967 75
Skylab **118**, *119*
slang **52**
Sleeper (film) 54
Smith, Hamilton O. 93
Smokey and the Bandit (film) **69**
Smokey the Bear **69**
solar power 65
Somoza family 73–74
South Vietnam, 6, 23, 24, 47–49. *See also* Vietnam War
Soviet Union 6, 7, 9, 23–24, 45, 46–47
space exploration 19, 47, **118**
Space Invaders 112, 113
Spassky, Boris 26
Spielberg, Steven 86
Spitz, Mark 29
sports 29, 31–32, 56, 69–71, 84–85
Sports Illustrated (magazine) 32
Spungen, Nancy **96**
stagflation 115, 121*g*
Stapleton, Ruth Carter **75**
Star Wars (film) 86
Starr, Edwin 13
Steinem, Gloria 15, **28**, 116
Stevens, Cat 55
Straits of Tirian 79
Strategic Arms Limitation Talks (SALT I) 26, **111**, 121*g*
Strategic Arms Limitations Talks (SALT II) **111**, 121*g*
streaking **55**
student protests 8
subway cars 113, 114
Sudan 30
Suez Canal 79
Sugar Hill Gang 112, 114, 115
Summer, Donna 95
Super Bowl 69
Superfly (film) **15**

Supreme Court, U.S. 14, 19
Surgeon General, U.S. 18, 27
Syria 30, 75

T

Taylor, James 55
television 27, 33, 52–53, **83**
Tenerife runway colission 80
tennis 31–32
test tube baby **93**
Texas Instruments 18
Tho, Le Duc 24
Thompson, David 70
Thompson, Hunter S. 36
Thompson, Linda *72*
Three Mile Island Nuclear
    Generating Station 99
Time (magazine) 32
toga parties **84**
Towering Inferno, The (film) 54
Trail of Broken Treaties 16, 17
Trans-Alaska Pipeline System 74
Twenty-sixth Amendment **9**

U

unemployment 33, 61, 63–64
University of Alabama 23
University of Michigan 51

V

Van Peebles, Melvin **15**
Van Thieu, Nguyen 48
Vance, Cyrus 77, 78
Vicious, Sid **96**

video games 33, 112–113
videotape cassette recorder
    (VCR) 46
Viet Cong 7, 47–49
Vietnam
    Chinese invasion of **101**
Vietnam Veterans Against the
    War 23
Vietnam War 6–7, 23–24, 35, 45,
    47–49, 82, **101**
    protests against *5*, 7, 8
Vietnamization 23, 121*g*
Viking space mission **64**
Village People 95
Virginia Squires 70
voting **9**
Voyager spacecraft **64**

W

Walkman 95
Wallace, George 21, 22, *23*, 34
Wallenda, Karl 98
Walton, Bill *70*
"War" (song) 13
Washington Post 35
Watergate scandal 35–37, 41, 45,
    50, 58, 82, 100, 121*g*
Watson, James 91
West Bank 75
Westmoreland, William C. *8*, 9
"What's Going On" (song) 13
"When We Grow Up" (song) 27
"whip inflation now" (WIN) 50
White, Kevin **25**

white supremacy **56**
Whole Earth Catalog 12
Wilson, Dick 17
Wolfe, Tom 82
women 5, 14, 51
    abortion 26–27, 91, 116
    African American 5, 6, 14,
        27
    feminism 15–16, 115, 117,
        120*g*
    liberation 15–16, 89–91, 117,
        121*g*
    military participation 16
    politicans 5, 6, 15, 89
Women's Tennis Association 32
Woodward, Bob 35
World Football League (WFL)
    69
World Hockey Association
    (WHA) 69, 71, 115
World Series 11, 29, 85
World Trade Center *20*
World War II, 31, 42, 50, 64. *See
    also* post–World War II
Wounded Knee 17, 51

Y

"YMCA" (song) 95
Yom Kippur War 30, 31, 75
Young, Andrew 59, **105**

Z

Zhou Enlai 25
Zoom (television show) 27